Faith-Based Reflections on *American Life*

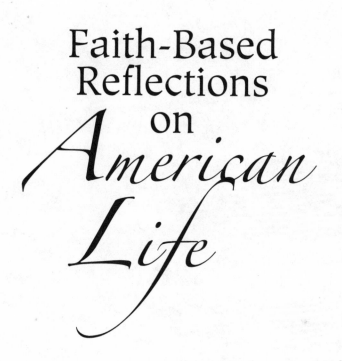

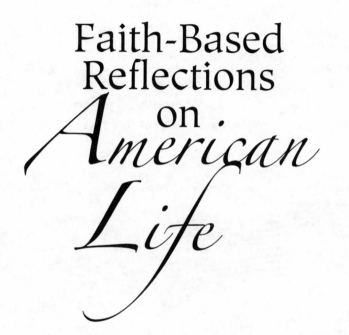

Faith-Based Reflections on American Life

WILLIAM J. BYRON, SJ

PAULIST PRESS
New York/Mahwah, NJ

Scripture texts in this work are taken from the *New American Bible with Revised New Testament* © 1991, 1986, 1970, Confraternity of Christian Doctrine, Washington, DC. and are used by the permission of the copyright owner. All rights reserved. No part of the *New American Bible* may be reproduced in any form without permission in writing from the copyright owner.

The Publisher gratefully acknowledges use of the following materials:

Excerpt from March 22, 1959, interview with Robert Frost in Reflection #7 on p. 19 from NBC's *Meet the Press* © 1959 by National Broadcasting Company, Inc. Used with permission.

Gratitude to Johnny Duhan for use of lyrics from "The Voyage" in Reflection # 9 on p. 24 with permission of the composer. Copyright © 1991 John Duhan. All rights reserved.

Gratitude to Samuel Hazo, Director of the International Poetry Forum in Pittsburgh, Pennsylvania, for permission to use his poems "Gene" in Reflection # 15 on p. 41 and "At the Site Memorial" in Reflection # 35 on p. 85.

Cover design by Sharyn Banks
Book design by Lynn Else

Copyright © 2010 by Corporation of Roman Catholic Clergymen

Library of Congress Cataloging-in-Publication Data

Byron, William J., 1927–
    Faith-based reflections on American life / William J. Byron.
      p. cm.
    ISBN 978-0-8091-4638-3 (alk. paper)
    1. Catholic Church. 2. Christian life—United States. 3. Christian life—Catholic authors. I. Title.
    BX4705.B997A5 2010
    282'.7309045—dc22

                                                                2009037247

Published by Paulist Press
997 Macarthur Boulevard
Mahwah, New Jersey 07430

www.paulistpress.com

Printed and bound in the United States of America

Contents

~

For
Martie and Bob Gillin
in faith and friendship through the years

Introduction

In 2001, David Gibson, then editor of Catholic News Service (CNS), invited me to write a biweekly general interest column for the CNS Syndicate. "Any topic, any theme," he said, "just try to observe our 600-word limit and don't overdo the spirituality; we have plenty of that already." He was referring, of course, to the themes typically developed by some of the writers who provide material for the electronic CNS package of columns that goes out each week from Washington to diocesan newspapers around the country and offshore to other English-speaking countries such as Australia and the United Kingdom.

The invitation was attractive so I agreed, and I remain grateful to David for the opportunity. He confided to me then that he was anticipating sooner rather than later the retirement of the great labor expert and social justice commentator Monsignor George V. Higgins, whose "Yardstick" column had for many years been a prominent part of the CNS package. I knew Monsignor Higgins well, admired his work, and was honored to fall in line behind him.

We decided to call my column "Looking Around." It has touched upon a wide-ranging list of topics that have caught my Catholic eye and engaged my Catholic mind. I've arranged these essays now in the categories that represent the nine parts of this book and updated them for current consumption. This book is, as the title indicates, a set of "faith-based" reflections and my faith, of course, is Catholic. It will, presumably, be of interest to the Catholic reader and perhaps to others as well.

I can claim that all of this is original material; I simply don't claim that all of it is new. I certainly hope that the reader will find it timely. This is a random-access book that can be read front to back, back to front, or at any thumb-stop in between.

Upon review, I've noticed that the range of topics is wide but not comprehensive; nothing on science, for example. That simply points to my limitations and perhaps to selective vision as I "look around" the Catholic world every other week. I had considered naming this book, *Full Circle: Looking All the Way Around*, but my writer's reach has been a bit short of a 360-degree sweep. I don't apologize for that, just acknowledge a limit on competence if not consciousness, although now that I've noticed some lacunae, I'll try to take a wider look for column material in the weeks and years ahead.

Still, here at the outset, the question has to be asked: Why pull those columns together now? Why would anyone want to read this book? My honest, if somewhat immodest reply is because the topics are timely and the book is interesting. In some cases, I've surprised myself by an ability to look around corners and see issues of emerging importance. Read on to see if you agree.

I suspect that this book will be passed around with certain sections tabbed for the attention of others in the family, or left on nightstands or coffee tables for others to pick up and read. Elders will want their offspring to see one essay or another, and it is conceivable that the young will tab a section or two for the attention of their parents. Spouses will want each other to share this insight or that; they'll find lots to talk about in this book.

I've occasionally quipped that the plural of anecdote is data. What I do often in these pages is spin out some anecdotes that produce interesting "data" that help to explain a lot of what's been happening over the past decade in the Catholic world that I inhabit. Fellow inhabitants will, I hope, find this book helpful in their ongoing effort to make sense of what is happening around them. They will also, I hope, find here some good material to fuel those conversations without which family ties weaken and even faith itself recedes from consciousness in the congestion and confusion of daily news.

PART ONE
Family

1. Mission Statement for a Marriage

My book, *Words at the Wedding*, focuses on commitment. It opens with an essay on sacrifice that resurrects an "exhortation" that used to be read at the beginning of every Catholic wedding in the Unites States. For a century before the 1960s, every bride and groom about to exchange their marriage vows in a Catholic wedding heard these words:

> Beloved of Christ. You are about to enter upon a union which is most sacred and most serious. It is most sacred, because established by God Himself. By it, He gave to man a share in the greatest work of creation, the work of the continuation of the human race. And in this way He sanctified human love and enabled man and woman to help each other live as children of God, by sharing a common life under His fatherly care.
>
> Because God himself is thus its author marriage is...a holy institution, requiring of those who enter into it a complete and unreserved giving of self. But Christ our Lord added to the holiness of marriage an even deeper meaning....He referred to the love of marriage to describe His own love for His Church....And so He gave to Christians a new

vision of what married life ought to be, a life of self-sacrificing love like His own....[Marriage], then, is most serious, because it will bind you together for life in a relationship so close and so intimate, that it will profoundly influence your whole future. That future, with its hopes and disappointments, its successes and its failures, its pleasures and its pains, its joys and its sorrows, is hidden from your eyes. You know that these elements are mingled in every life, and are to be expected in your own. And so not knowing what is before you, you take each other for better or for worse, for richer or for poorer, in sickness and in health, until death.

Truly, then, these words are most serious. It is a beautiful tribute to your undoubted faith in each other, that recognizing their full import, you are, nevertheless, so willing and ready to pronounce them....It is most fitting that you rest the security of your wedded life upon the great principle of self-sacrifice....Henceforth you will...be one in mind, one in heart, and one in affections. And whatever sacrifices you may hereafter be required to make to preserve this mutual life, always make them generously. Sacrifice is usually difficult and irksome. Only love can make it easy, and perfect love can make it a joy....God so loved the world that He gave His only-begotten Son, and the Son so loved us that He gave Himself for our salvation....

No greater blessing can come to your married life than pure conjugal love, loyal and true to the end. May, then, this love with which you join your hands and hearts today never fail, but grow deeper and stronger as the years go on. And if true love and the unselfish spirit of perfect sacrifice guide your every action, you can expect the greatest measure of earthly happiness that may be allotted to man in this vale of tears. The rest is in the hands of God. Nor will God be wanting to your needs; He will pledge you the life-long support of His graces in the holy sacrament which you are now going to receive.

These wise words are worth repeating whenever wedding bells ring. I used them as a reflection/prayer in the opening session of our several-times-a-year, six-week marriage preparation course when I was a pastor in Washington, DC. Without fail, two or three of the couples asked that I use them again in their actual wedding ceremony. I often did. And I usually suggested that the newlyweds find a calligrapher friend who could put those words on parchment, suitable for framing, and let them hang as a mission statement in the home that would house the family their marriage would produce.

2. Spousal Support in Stressful Times

An often unexamined presupposition, in these days of widespread agreement that men and women are equal, is the mistaken conclusion that men and women are identical. They are not, of course, and there are emotional and psychological differences that require special attention when either a husband or wife might be unemployed and looking for work, and his or her spouse wants to be supportive. The transition period could be stressful. Here's a word of advice to married job seekers from a construction company executive who, together with his wife, successfully weathered the transition: "Leave the advice-giving to others outside the marriage relationship; it may be perceived as criticism. View the crisis as an opportunity to be vulnerable with your spouse and thus strengthen the marriage." Those are wise words.

Both men and women at all stages of their lives experience varying degrees of discouragement and loneliness, emotions easily activated by job loss. The male, however, is more bothered by and sensitive to discouragement, while the female tends to be more often beset with loneliness than with a feeling of failure. This is not to say women do not feel discouraged at times, or that men do not experience loneliness. They clearly do. I have observed, however, that men tend to be more achievement-oriented and women more relational in their approach to work and life. Again, this is not to say that women have no drive to achieve and men are uninterested in forging relationships.

What I am getting at is this: there appears to be a male propensity toward discouragement and a female propensity toward loneliness. Their psychological vulnerabilities differ because their psychological propensities differ. Failure to achieve can activate discouragement; a failed relationship can trigger loneliness. Whether these propensities are genetically rooted and unalterable is not my question to pursue. I simply remark that, generally speaking, different tendencies are there. In my experience, an awareness of the difference can enable spouses or friends to draw closer to one another by permitting their psychological complementarity to come into play. It works this way.

The male needs encouragement in the face of an abiding (it has been there all along, not just in a moment of career crisis!) sense of inadequacy, self-doubt, and a propensity toward discouragement. The female needs the presence of

someone who cares, along with the conversation, consideration, and attention that the caring person can bring. This
provides her with emotional security—a sense of being connected—in the face of a propensity toward loneliness.

If each is attentive to the deeper psychological need of
the other, each will enhance the likelihood of having his or
her own psychological need met. The wife who gives encouragement, praise, and personal reassurance to her discouraged spouse, makes herself a significantly more attractive
target for the attentive presence she needs and wants. In
stressful circumstances, like those surrounding unexpected
job loss, criticism and resentment from a wife will repel the
husband, deepen his sense of failure, and create a chasm
rather than a union between the spouses. Similarly, if the
wife is the victim of job loss, insensitivity on the part of the
husband will only aggravate the relational failure, the feeling
of disconnectedness, and the concomitant loneliness.

Sensitivity can strengthen the relationship and hasten a
successful conclusion to the job search.

3. The Line between
Trust and Neglect

One Saturday morning I spent a few hours with about sixty
high school boys and girls and their parents listening to them
talk about better parent-teen communication regarding sex,
alcohol, and drugs. The question for parents that kept pop-
ping into my mind as I listened to both sides speak was
"Where does trust end and neglect begin?"

The teenagers want to be trusted. The parents want to
trust. But parental unease surfaces as the potential for parental

neglect in the face of possibly unwise and risky teenage behavior rises. Where do you draw the line between trust and neglect? Surely, no parent wants to be guilty of neglect, just as all parents want to trust their offspring. The question provides a nice framework for great conversations, if both parents and teenagers are willing to talk. Doing it in groups with other parents and teens seems to improve the acoustics for the desired exchange.

The conversation, as I heard it, turned on issues of curfew, driving (who's in the car? who's at the wheel? where are you going?), friends (who do you hang out with?), honesty, pregnancy, the Internet, and trust. In families, the participants seemed to agree, there is a need for "consistency" and there has to be agreement on the "irreversibles" in the ongoing discussions about "boundaries."

Communication is, of course, at the heart of dealing with these issues. The teens have to be permitted to speak up openly about what they perceive to be double standards (for example, some parents drink and drive). Parents have to explain their "need to verify" (for example, call the parents of a teen who is hosting the party).

Expert facilitators were on hand to provide technical information on drugs and alcohol. It was helpful to dig a bit for answers to the question of why kids drink—to have fun, try to cope, or just see what it's like? Similarly with drugs.

Notably absent from the conversation was any reference to religion (although all four of the schools represented were Catholic). Nor was much said about the need to establish baseline respect for human dignity. That would cover respect for self as well as others as a bedrock principle of right, fair, and just behavior. I also noticed that no one suggested the value of service projects in getting teens "out of themselves" and into growth-producing character development. Not that participants were unaware of this; they just didn't bring it up.

No mention was made of shared work—parents and teens working together on meaningful projects. That used to happen a generation or two ago when it was not uncommon for a small-scale family business to provide Saturday and summer employment for the kids. Those opportunities produced for the young a lot more than spending money.

It is also worth noting that the one school that hosted the gathering and the other three that participated had very little to do with the design, promotion, and provision of the program. This was the work of one mother whose children are all grown with families of their own. She decided that it would be useful and just went ahead and put it all together.

It would be too facile to say that anyone could do it. But it is not wide of the mark to suggest that this intergenerational exchange of experience and information could be happening on a much larger scale if more good people step up and decide to make it happen.

4. A Mother's Message on AIDS

As I write, an estimated thirty-three million people around the world are living with the AIDS virus. For the past quarter century, HIV/AIDS has been in and out of the headlines. Recently, however, according to an editorial in the *New York Times*, "AIDS appears to be making an alarming comeback. *The Journal of the American Medical Association* reports that the incidence of the HIV infection among gay men is shooting up, following an encouraging period of decline."

When the AIDS epidemic first broke out, the mother of a young gay man who died of complications related to AIDS wondered aloud to me, "What if my son had learned to say no more firmly to himself as he moved through the developmental years on his way to saying yes to life?" She had tried, she said, to teach all her children the value of self-denial and that it is perfectly all right not to act on every impulse and satisfy every urge. "Why are we afraid to say this," she asked, "as we look at our young and worry about AIDS?

"I just wish my son had used his freedom better, more wisely, more humbly, and with the courage that sustained him through his terminal illness." Then she added, "During long and painful watches at his bedside when he lay dying at home, I found myself wondering how many unknown others had been infected by him. That's an awful thought, I know, but there it was. I also lamented the pitiful and fatal exchange he unwisely made for the experience of a few pleasurable moments. I still wonder. I still lament."

Multiply those musings by any number approaching the thirty-three million alive today and infected by the AIDS virus, and you have the makings of a case waiting to be made by parents and educators to the unsuspecting young. It is a case for self-denial—not the only defense against AIDS, to be sure, but one available to all and, for many, waiting to be tried.

AIDS can infect the selfless and selfish, the virtuous and the profligate, gay and straight, male and female. Exposure to the risk will differ, depending on free choices and the luck of the draw. Blood transfusions and open cuts are the avenues of entry used by this killer virus in attacking those victims we tend to regard as "the innocent." Tainted needles and sexually transmitted body fluids deliver the virus to others whom the "righteous ones" among us dismiss heartlessly as having gotten exactly what they deserved.

Perhaps nature is unforgiving of those who tamper with its laws, but God, the author of nature, is nothing if not forgiving and faithful. That's why the mother I've been quoting is a woman of hope. Whenever she gets the chance, she talks to the young about AIDS.

"I tell them what they may have heard already from others: 'If you get into bed with someone, you should realize that you are in bed with everyone that person has ever had before.' I don't disguise my values; I urge them to locate theirs. I tell them, 'It is okay not to act on every impulse and satisfy every urge, It is okay—even cool—to deny yourself. Self-denial is not stony-faced stoicism,' I tell them. It is, I say, their first clue to the meaning of love and the mystery of a long and happy life."

5. A Mother's Way of the Cross

I was fairly well along in years—about age sixty, I guess—when I received a letter from an elderly nun who said I would not know her, but that she remembered seeing me as a young child.

She was writing from Camilla Hall, the retirement community and assisted-living facility for the Immaculate Heart of Mary (IHM) sisters in suburban Philadelphia. What prompted her to write, she said, was that she had seen my photograph and name in print occasionally and it always reminded her of the days when she was a very young nun assigned to teach in the parochial school of the parish where I lived. The parish church (Immaculate Conception in the Germantown section of Philadelphia) was large and architecturally impressive, she reminded me. She recalled seeing my mother, a young widow, with two preschool toddlers in hand (my older brother and me), making the Stations of the Cross there.

Those were the Depression years. Religious faith was strong in our neighborhood, but economic insecurity was widespread. Some neighbors lost their homes. Others had difficulty paying bills. Some few had trouble putting food on the table. But neighborhood life was positive, even happy, due in no small measure to our vibrant Vincentian parish with its excellent parochial school.

The point this retired sister wanted to make with me was the fact that she drew strength as a young nun in meeting her commitment to a religious vocation by simply seeing my mother make the Stations of the Cross.

Lent is the usual time for many to renew their commitment to discipleship by retracing the Way of the Cross, not in order to be seen by others—although there is something to be said for that—but simply to impress upon themselves the meaning of discipleship and the importance of the words, "If anyone would come after me, he must deny himself and take up his cross daily and follow me" (Luke 9:23).

I once gave a youth retreat to about seventy-five high school-age boys and girls in Bethel, Alaska. We had talks and liturgies in the parish church, and discussions and games in the parish hall. I wanted to encourage the teens to walk with the Lord in prayer as he made his Way of the Cross, but I noticed that the Stations were mounted high on the side walls of the church, certainly out of reach and practically out of sight of the kids. I suggested to the pastor that he might consider lowering them to a shoulder-high level where anyone on a prayerful walk within the walls of the church could see the path that Jesus took, look into the faces of those who accompanied him, friend and foe alike, and resolve to follow him more closely on their own walk through life.

In Houston, Texas, on the campus of the University of St. Thomas, there is a beautiful chapel with unusual Stations of the Cross. They are all indentations or insets on a side wall. The figures are, in effect, scooped out of the wall; only the impressions remain to guide the devotion of those who pause to pray.

Lent in its own devotional way is a pause to pray. But a pause at each of the Stations at any time of year can renew one's commitment to discipleship. And that, I think, is something I can surely say I learned from my mother, although I don't remember learning it and she never spelled it out in words.

6. Letter from Heaven

Not only is a pastor's work never done; it sometimes requires power tools not found in the pastor's ordinary tool kit. Six months after leaving my job as pastor of Holy Trinity in Washington, DC, I received a request from the parish school principal asking me to write a letter from heaven to one of her third graders.

This youngster, who had transferred into the third grade after I left Washington, was having a lot of difficulty adjusting to his father's recent death. His teacher gave an assignment requiring the children to write a letter to "someone who has had a significant influence" in their lives. This child chose to write to his father, whom he knew to be in heaven, from whom he expected an answer, and for whose return to earth he was praying every day.

The principal knew that I had lost my dad at a very early age and thought that I might be able to fill the bill. Here is what I wrote:

> Dear Robert (or, maybe I should be calling you "Bob" or "Bobby!"):
>
> I don't think we have ever met. I was pastor of Holy Trinity for the past three years and used to visit your school often. But you have a new pastor now and I'm down here in New Orleans filling in for a while as president of Loyola University.
>
> I wanted to write to you because you and I have a lot in common. When I was just a little boy, my father died and, of course, my mother told me when I was your age and started asking about him, that my dad was home with God in heaven. Like you, I wanted him here with me on earth, but that just was not to be.
>
> I've heard that you and each of your classmates have written letters to someone who has made a difference in your lives. You've written to your father and are hoping for an answer from heaven. You will receive an answer, but not in an envelope with a stamp on it that the mailman can deliver to your house. Your answer will come in the form of smiles and encouragement from grownups, a pat on the back from your teachers and coaches, and in quiet moments of happiness that God will bring unexpectedly into your heart. When the breeze

touches your cheek, imagine that your father's hand is touching you. When the sun shines on your face, remember that he is smiling on you. And when the stars come out at night, look up to the heavens and say hello to your dear dad.

You can be sure of this, my friend: your father loves you very much and would never have wanted to leave you, but it was just time for him to go home to God. You didn't do anything wrong to lose him; he just had to leave this world earlier than he wanted to. You love him, I know, and you would not want him not to be enjoying the eternal happiness of heaven. Still, it is okay to miss him and wish that he were here with you. From his place in heaven, he prays for you, your mother, and the two other children in your family. You can pray to your dad when you are happy or sad. You can tell him about your hopes and dreams. And you can honor his memory by growing up to be the kind of fellow that he would be very proud of. You and your family are in my prayers.

Peace!

7. From Big Russ, to Tim, to Luke: The Gift of Magnanimity

The sudden death of Tim Russert on June 13, 2008, brought the nation to its knees to mourn the loss of a great journalist whom most of the mourners had never met but all considered a friend.

Under his smiling face on the memorial card distributed at his funeral in Washington's Holy Trinity Catholic Church were words he often spoke: "The best exercise for the human heart is to bend over and pick someone else up." Ironically, a heart attack took his life; it was an enlarged heart, the autopsy revealed, made ever larger, I believe, by countless works of charity.

Big Russ and Me, Tim Russert's book-length salute to his dad, ends with a short letter to his son Luke. Love in both directions—for his father and his son—is palpable in the pages of this book. It enjoyed an upsurge in sales after Tim died. Anyone who reads it will find practical wisdom, political history, and a lot of laughs.

Tim Russert's wife Maureen Orth launched a book of her own in the same month that *Big Russ and Me* hit the bookstores. Hers is *The Importance of Being Famous: Behind the Scenes of the Celebrity-Industrial Complex*. It's a collection of essays, previously published in *Vanity Fair*, on celebrities ranging from Tina Turner to Dame Margot Fonteyn, with chapters in between on Madonna, Gerry Adams, Vladimir Putin, Mohamed Fayed, Michael Jackson, and other notables. Reading this book gives you a front-row seat at the media circus generated by the cable news channels' need to fill the air all day long, seven days a week.

My interest in these books stemmed from the fact that the Russerts were members of the parish in Georgetown where I used to be pastor. "If it's Sunday, it's *Meet the Press*," Tim would say to an audience of millions every week, so he wasn't often seen in the pews at Holy Trinity. But every Saturday afternoon at 4:00 he was in the nearby Georgetown University Hospital Chapel for the anticipated Sunday Mass. His book helped me to understand why.

"The most important thing that happened to me after [my wedding] was the birth of our son. We were living on the upper West Side of New York, and at 3 a.m. on August 22, 1985, Maureen went into labor." Tim took her to Lenox Hill Hospital.

> It was a long difficult labor....After a few hours I went outside for a breath of air. When I found myself in front of a church behind the hospital, I went in and knelt down at a little shrine to St. Anne, the mother of Mary and the patron saint of mothers. I prayed for a healthy baby and a healthy mother and vowed that I would never again miss Sunday Mass....When they brought me our nine-pound, thirteen-ounce baby and put him in my arms, I burst into tears....I knew that something magnificent and miraculous had happened....But there was so much I didn't yet know, and I couldn't possibly know. I whispered to Luke, "Never has a Papa loved a baby so much." I had no idea how much love I was capable of feeling for another human being. (*Big Russ and Me*, p. 290)

Russert later worried that "parents of my generation have often failed their kids. We are so eager to be understanding and sympathetic that we end up being too lenient."

Curiously, it was on *Meet the Press* in 1959, when Tim Russert was just a kid, that poet Robert Frost was asked by then moderator Lawrence Spivak about young people of that day. I have that interview tucked away in my files. Tim had retrieved it for me from the NBC archives.

> Question: "Do you think they are better than their fathers or grandfathers?"

Reply: "They won't be if they are made too comfortable and have their life too easy. We are like a rich father who wishes he knew how to give his son the hardships that made the father such a man."

Tim Russert's father, Big Russ, had the hardships; they are recounted in detail in the book *Big Russ and Me*. From Big Russ, Tim learned *magnanimity*, the word Robert Frost used on *Meet the Press* to describe the "most important thing" a father can pass on to his son. That's what Tim and Maureen did their best to pass on to Luke, who graduated from Boston College just weeks before his father died.

It was with an especially heavy heart that I offered Mass for Tim shortly after hearing the news of his death. The adjectives just aren't there to do justice to the description his person, personality, character, and commitment deserve. When *Meet the Press* suddenly became "Meet Your Maker" on that June afternoon, I'm confident that Tim heard the words we all hope to hear, "Well done, my good and faithful servant, enter into the home prepared for you from the foundation of the world." He belongs there; not because he was famous, but because he was a great family man. Tim Russert responded generously to his vocation, his calling, to be son, husband, and father—a holy trinity all its own.

8. *Bella:* The Beautiful Choice

At the Toronto Film Festival there are several awards. One is the Film Critics Award. Another is the People's Choice Award. What's the difference? I really don't know; I can only speculate. The "people's choice" probably has something to do with what ordinary viewers really like. The "film critics"

view the silver screen from a higher perch through a sophis-
ticated, if not elitist lens. I suspect the experts often miss
what the ordinary moviegoers, closer to the ground, connect
with eye-to-eye and heart-to-heart.

Well, *Bella* won the People's Choice Award in Toronto
for 2007, but when the film opened nationwide, the critics
for the *New York Times, Washington Post, Variety,* other
newspapers, Internet blogs, and slick magazines managed to
mute their enthusiasm.

"Bella" is the name of a sweet young child who shows
up in the last reel of this film to meet her tearful mother who
chose life over the alternative of an abortion several years
before. Neither the tears nor the life choice seem to have reg-
istered with the critics. They do register, however, with the
PG-13 audiences that filled the theaters to see this show.

I personally prefer realistic over impressionistic visual
art. I have to confess that the jumps and cuts in both story
line and visual flow left me momentarily confused from time
to time as I watched this stunning story unfold on the screen.
The crisis is indeed drawn with sufficient clarity for the
viewer at the line of choice that a young, unmarried, pregnant woman has to face between having an abortion or bear-
ing a child.

There is no didacticism here. There is no propaganda,
much less preaching. There is, however, quiet persuasion on
the part of a handsome young man whose earlier misfortune
behind the wheel of a sports car resulted in the accidental
death of a child. He befriends the pregnant woman without
the benefit of any romantic links to her.

What struck me as I sat engaged and enthralled by this
ninety-one-minute experience of film art was how much

more effective persuasion can be over coercion in the abortion debate.

Threats, condemnation, and heavy-handed coercion represent the wrong way to go on the pro-life path. Nonjudgmental acceptance and support of the woman who has to make the choice, and gentle persuasion from someone ready, able, and willing to care for the child, are surely more effective ways to reach the right solution.

There are good words spoken for adoption in a sidebar plot to this family-focused film. There is much more here to think about and nothing to resent. No finger-pointing, no name-calling, no criminalization. There is just selfless love (is there any other kind?) and human reassurances that demonstrate how being with, as well as for, a troubled person can bring light out of darkness and hope out of despair.

When the film vacated the theaters and became available on DVD, I encouraged parents to view it at home with their teenagers (not easy to do, I discovered) and discuss it afterward with the help of questions like these:

What does it mean to choose?

How can one choose wisely?

How important are friends in encouraging wise choices?

Choices are made every day in all areas of life. What are the important life choices you will have to make?

What does courage have to do with choosing well and wisely?

Although you will always be alone with the consequences of your choice—it's yours and no one else's—you never have to be alone in preparing for and living with your choice.

9. Happy Anniversary Time

If "love is what you've been through with someone," wedding anniversaries have a way of tempering idealism with the realism (the day-to-day, year-in-and-year-out, practical, down-to-earth, "being through") of marriage. "Would you do it all over again?" is a question not for the faint of heart; it could ruin the anniversary celebration! Very few, if any, couples I know would have anything but a strong affirmative answer to that question. They've been blessed, and they are grateful. And so they celebrate when anniversary time rolls around.

The famous jurist Benjamin N. Cardozo, when officiating at a wedding in 1931, said:

> Three great mysteries there are in the lives of mortal beings: the mystery of birth at the beginning; the mystery of death at the end; and, greater than either, the mystery of love. Everything that is most precious in life is a form of love. (Cited in John T. Noonan, Jr.'s review of *Cardozo* by Andrew L. Kauffman in the *New York Times*, January 21, 1998)

Thinking back on love and marriage from an anniversary perspective can indeed produce inspiring words. But anniversary time also opens the reflective mind to the real struggles any marriage project entails. Marriage takes a lot of work. How satisfying, therefore, to look back with gratitude at the whole project when any anniversary of an intact marriage is celebrated!

Anniversaries unlock the sorrows together with the joys and, as most anniversary celebrants will smilingly admit, the joys redeem the sorrows every time.

That's the way it has been for Martie and Bob Gillin, friends of mine since high school days. I was in the seminary when they were married, but I've officiated at the weddings of five of their children and assisted at the funeral of one son. Martie and Bob heard a priest say to them in the opening "exhortation" in their own wedding ceremony in 1957 that their future "with its hopes and disappointments, its successes and its failures, its pleasures and its pains, its joys and its sorrows, is hidden from your eyes. You know that these elements are mingled in every life, and are to be expected in your own." All those elements have been part of the Gillin family experience.

So with Martie and Bob in mind now that they've celebrated their fiftieth, I recall words from a song that I incorporated into the homily I gave at the wedding of their son Steve and his bride Leslie in 1999. The words are from the song "Voyage" by Johnny Duhan:

> Life is an ocean
> and love is a boat
> In troubled waters,
> it keeps you afloat.
> When we started the voyage,
> there was just me and you.
> Gathered around us,
> we now have a crew.

The "crew" of family gives us the security and support we need on our transit through life. What a joy it is to have the crew gather round for those anniversary celebrations that come in the evening of life when the voyage is closer to the end than to the beginning, and, thanks be to God, the marriage is still afloat!

The crew members—the kids—get both example and instruction from parents who agree to renew their vows in the presence of children and grandchildren at the anniversary celebration. That's an opportunity not to be missed. The "for better or worse, richer or poorer, in sickness and health" dimensions of the marriage commitment, with its "until death do us part" declaration, constitute powerful prose that holds the promise of additional anniversary joy for generations to come.

PART TWO
Interesting Individuals

10. Trevor Armbrister: Dying Gratefully

My friend Trevor Armbrister died of pancreatic cancer at age 73. He was a retired senior editor at *Reader's Digest* and had earlier worked as editor of the *Saturday Evening Post*. He was an investigative reporter and author of many books, including one on President Gerald Ford.

I first met Trevor in connection with "Christmas in April," a community-service all-volunteer initiative he led in the Washington, DC, area to repair and rehabilitate housing for the poor. One of his Christmas-in-April colleagues contacted me to say that Trevor was seriously ill and that he would appreciate a call from me.

"I'm an Episcopalian," he reminded me when we made telephone contact, "and I'm not planning to convert, but I'd really like to talk to you." He knew he was going to die and wanted to discuss the process and get some advice on how to prepare, especially, how to say good-bye.

I had at that time a book manuscript ready to go to the publisher. It was titled *A Book of Quiet Prayer: For All the Seasons, Stages, Moods, and Circumstances of Life*. One of the "circumstances" is illness, another is death. I told him I'd send the manuscript as an e-mail attachment, hoping it might be helpful.

When I went to his home in the Maryland suburbs of Washington on a sunny winter morning, there was a print-out of the manuscript on a coffee table. I noticed some red-pen editorial markups and marginal notes, along with a list of questions. Next to the manuscript he placed a small tape recorder. "Do you mind if I record?" he asked. "I'm a writer and reporter, you know, and this time I'm the story."

Trevor's wife Judy gracefully and diplomatically found other things she had to do outside the home at that hour, so he and I were alone, with his tiny tape recorder, to reflect together in faith and friendship.

From the book's opening chapter, "Through the Years," Trevor lifted and repeated this line: "Light and darkness are the scissors that divide our days one from another and thus prepare them for packaging into months and years." The text goes on to say that the years are then packaged into decades and thus a life span is produced—all as a result of the division of light from darkness. Trevor and I then talked about light and darkness, giving him the opportunity to praise Judy, the "shining light" of his life and his gentle strength in his final illness.

He related well to another prayer in that manuscript and found himself praying: "'I believe; help my unbelief' I find these words from Mark's Gospel reassuring,/ and so I make them my own, as I come out of my personal darkness/ toward you, Lord, the everlasting Light."

I told Trevor that in my view, the essential content of all religion can be reduced to one word—*gratitude*. Breathe in God's gifts, God's goodness to you, and then breathe out your expression of thanks, I told him. On a sickbed you can wrap yourself in a blanket of *gratias*, I said. Let gratitude protect you from anxiety, discouragement, inner loneliness.

Trevor liked this and was able to say, in the words of another prayer in this book of "quiet" prayer, "I could start counting now, Lord,/ and I would be at it for days taking inventory of your blessings to me./…I pray for an abiding sense of gratitude./ One word turns my heart to you: *gratias*!" And just a short time later that one word sent him home to God.

Judy asked me to give the homily at Trevor's funeral in St. Columba's Episcopal Church in northwest Washington. She also asked me to carry the urn containing his ashes and place it in his niche in the columbarium wall outside the church. I did so with a heavy but grateful heart.

And now on those occasions when I drive by, I think of Trevor, say a prayer, lift a sad salute, and simply say, "*Gratias*."

11. Dick Cass: Not All Pro Football Heroes Are on the Field

For most of my adult years, I've had a love-hate relationship with professional football. As a youngster, I thrilled, in those pre-television days, to the on-field accomplishments of Bert Bell's Philadelphia Eagles.

In preseason practice before my senior year in high school in 1944, my St. Joseph's Prep teammates and I were in "camp" together with the Philadelphia Eagles for two weeks in August at what was then known as West Chester State Teachers College, now West Chester University. We worked out in full equipment in the morning while the Eagles did light drills in T-shirts and shorts. In the afternoon, we scrimmaged as they, with no assigned practice of their own, stood by to offer advice—their backs with our backs, their ends with ours, right down the line. And in the evening, we watched them scrimmage under the lights. They occupied the lower floors of the same dorm that housed all of us for those two memorable weeks.

Those were the days before the big bucks changed just about everything—scheduling, salaries, franchises, ticket prices, broadcasting, size, speed, and intensity of the game, not to mention players' attitudes toward and accessibility to young kids. Commercialization, not professionalism, was setting in. In any case, my interest in the pro game began to wane.

Even the college game was changing, I thought; players were all on their way to the pros and, in my view, commitment to the books took a distant back seat to anticipation of the big signing bonuses. Falling graduation rates were further indicators of decline. I began to think of the Army–Navy game as the sole surviving genuinely collegiate gridiron contest in America.

As a Jesuit seminarian in the Baltimore area in the late 1950s, I became a Colts fan when Johnny Unitas and his teammates made football history. I worked in New Orleans in the early 1970s, when the Saints played their home games in Tulane Stadium, where I saw many an enjoyable game as quarterback Archie Manning, father of today's NFL star quarterbacks Peyton and Eli, was doing his heroic best to prevent public opinion from forcing the franchise to change its name from Saints to Martyrs. Subsequent exposure to the Redskins when I spent many years in Washington served to keep me connected to "The Game."

More recently, in connection with research for a book on business ethics, I ran across this interesting definition of character in an account of how the National Football League runs a training camp for rookies in an effort to protect them from various forms of self-destruction. The players are told that "character is what you do when you are angry, afraid, or bored...and no one is watching."

Well, I hope the NFL rookies and veterans alike took notice when Dick Cass, president of the Baltimore Ravens, while no one was watching, donated a kidney in 2006 to a longtime friend and law school classmate. Weeks later, a headline on the sports page of the *Baltimore Sun* read: "Donation from Ravens' Cass Gives an Old Friend Gift of Life."

A transplant surgeon remarked that donors like Cass "are the closest things to heroes on this earth that you are going to meet." Mr. Cass, whose name was in the early mix of potential candidates to succeed Paul Tagliabue as NFL commissioner, modestly said, "I did some reading and found it wasn't that big a deal. The surgery isn't fun, but other than that, you don't need two kidneys."

Dick Cass has given a compelling example of selflessness in a culture too often characterized by arrogance, power, and me-first greed. In saving the life of a friend, he has helped restore my love and respect for "The Game."

12. Andy McGowan: A Salesman for the Lord

"I'm in sales, not management," was Monsignor Andrew J. McGowan's immediate response to anyone who looked to him to bring divine power to bear on any crisis, real or imagined. His lighthearted quips eased the anxieties of air travelers, job seekers, test takers, or others who turned to him to "do something" in anxious moments.

Monsignor McGowan, who was "Father Joe" to family and close friends, and "Andy" to countless others, was a priest of the Diocese of Scranton. He died at age eighty from complications following cardiac surgery. For many years this best known and most beloved clergyman in Northeastern Pennsylvania was much in demand for invocations at public functions and a sought-after toastmaster at testimonial dinners. In that capacity he shared space on the dais on several occasions with Bob Hope. He once introduced Hope with so many one-liners of his own that he forgot to say the invocation he was there to offer. So when Bob Hope took the microphone, he bowed his head and said, "Now let us pray." Mr. Hope on another occasion urged him to "do something religious—like take up a collection!"

I first met Andrew McGowan in 1975 when I became president of the University of Scranton and he served there on the board of trustees. He was then rector of the minor seminary in the diocese and responsible for the program of spiritual formation, but the seminarians did their academic work at the University. He was also outside chairman of the town's only Catholic hospital where he maintained an office. We used to joke that he was the ecclesiastical equivalent of the Maytag repairman and thus free to serve on countless boards, be a goodwill ambassador for the diocese, represent the bishop on the Pennsylvania Catholic Conference, and chair multiple fund-raising efforts for community causes.

Years ago, when the priest-secretary to the long-time Bishop of Scranton was ordained an auxiliary bishop, a dinner for all priests working in the diocese followed the ordination ceremony. Naturally, Monsignor McGowan was the toastmaster. "Well, we all move up a notch now," he told his fellow clerics. And in the presence of the gentle, dignified, rather elderly bishop, he reported that people around town were asking "What's the difference between an auxiliary bishop and a bishop?" "I tell them about six months," he quipped, and then turned to the veteran prelate and said, "Don't worry, Your Excellency, we worship the very quicksand you walk on!"

He agreed to take a seat on the forty-two-member board (composition half lay, half clergy, most of whom were bishops) of The Catholic University of America while I was president there from 1982–92. At one memorable meeting, immediately after chairman Cardinal Joseph Bernardin welcomed Cardinals John O'Connor and Bernard Law back from Rome where they had just received their red hats, Monsignor McGowan piped up, "One of you fellows has gone as far as you can go!"

In 1978, when he subjected himself to a public "roasting" at a dinner that launched the United Way's annual fundraising drive in Lackawanna County, Monsignor McGowan fended off the friendly barbs and bullets long enough to say, "Nonsense and laughter are very important to a community. Lord, preserve us from being too solemn, or severe, or pretentious. Humor is the sign of the best of our humanity. You don't find any laughter in prejudice, no joy in intolerance. Where there is a rigid and closed mind, there is no smile. Humor brushes us with a touch of humility that we all need."

Humility and humor were his in abundance; may he now have eternal love, joy, and peace.

13. Horace McKenna: Apostle to the Poor, Friend of the Needy

On a mid-May Saturday afternoon in 2007, several hundred Washington, DC-area Catholics—lay, religious, and clergy—gathered to mark the twenty-fifth anniversary of the death of Jesuit Father Horace McKenna (1899–1982). He was an apostle to the poor who fed the hungry and sheltered the homeless while urging others to come up with permanent solutions to these problems. Immediate care for Washington's hungry and homeless continues today in the McKenna Center in the basement of the church on North Capitol Street where this good pastor worked.

Father McKenna expressed his solidarity with the poor by sleeping occasionally in homeless shelters and eating in soup kitchens without separating himself from his Jesuit community. He once told me that he tried for awhile to get along without wearing underwear just to be closer to the poor, but that proved not to be such a good idea. "We're middle class," he said, "and we have to be if we're going to be around long enough to help the poor."

Those who gathered at St. Aloysius Church in Washington wanted to celebrate his life and search for ways to extend his influence, particularly in the national capital area, through advocacy and relief for the hungry and homeless. As one who knew and admired Horace McKenna, I'd like to let him speak here in his own words:

> "If the Church does not care for the poor, they will be neglected. That is the test of our faithfulness to Christ: how we relate to the poor."

"I really believe that every person is a revelation of God—the joy of God, the love of God. I feel that the human person on the street is the appearance of Jesus Christ consumed with human needs."

"The poor are here, I believe, to teach us that we must live modestly."

"The Church without social work is like Christ without miracles."

"Our Lord did his miracles instantaneously at a word, but his Church—his brothers, his sisters, his fathers and mothers—have to do their miracles slowly."

"The poor can't lift themselves up by their own bootstraps because they have no boots."

"I think we need to have marches—hunger marches, marches for the homeless, marches for peace. We need to make the government realize it should not spend our food money on armaments for war."

Whether or not there will be marches on Washington in an effort to extend the McKenna legacy is anybody's guess. There will, I suspect, be strategic planning to organize alumni of Washington-area Jesuit schools and parishioners from the two Jesuit parishes in the national capital to make something happen in providing food and housing for the poor.

Early in the decade of the 1960s, with nudging and encouragement from Father McKenna, the Washington, DC, chapter of the Georgetown University Alumni Association used its corporate clout to facilitate the federally funded construction of the 199-unit Sursum Corda low-income housing project just a few blocks from Capitol Hill. Those units are now owned by the residents in a limited equity partnership. Private developers are offering to buy out the present residents to make room for an enlargement of capacity and reorganization of ownership that will result in many more market-rate units and far fewer subsidized housing units for the poor.

Although Horace McKenna is no longer around to speak up for the poor, it is likely that some influential Washingtonians, who are part of the Jesuit network and remember Father McKenna as a friend of the needy, will try to make his voice heard in policy debates that will affect some of today's poor in whom Horace McKenna would see "the appearance of Jesus Christ consumed with human needs."

The face of low-income housing in the nation's capital will undoubtedly change and it is likely to change for the worse unless there are eyes, like those of Horace McKenna, that can see the likeness of Christ in the faces of the poor.

14. Diane Sherwood: Celebrating Life

Diane Sherwood is the only person I know who could have pulled it off. Forced by cancer to leave her job as associate director of the Washington Interfaith Conference, in 2002, she underwent treatment at the Washington Hospital Center. When advised that chemotherapy could do no more for her, and that no other treatment would work, she told me with a smile, "I'm going home to die."

As Diane's pastor at Holy Trinity Catholic Church in Georgetown, I gave her the sacrament of the sick, the anointing with holy oil accompanied by prayers for her return to health, if God so willed. Or, if it was time for her to leave this world, the anointing was intended to give her strength to bear any loneliness or fear that might touch her during her final days. At home, friends came to pray. Both Diane and they talked about planning her funeral. Then an idea came to her: "Why not a celebration of life before I die? Not my life, but the gift of life and friendship. Let's do it in an inter-faith setting." Since the promotion of interreligious under-standing was an important part of her life, it was not surprising to hear Diane say,

> Something new is breaking open. We're coming together in our day to create new bonds of inter-faith friendship; we are finding new ways of part-nering.

So, on Labor Day, 2002, at four o'clock in the afternoon, several hundred people, about one-third of them Trinity parishioners, gathered at Tifereth Israel Synagogue for a "Celebration of Life." Diane was there at the center of it all.

The prelude was the Gayatri Mantra Chant, a favorite of Diane's. The president of the synagogue welcomed everyone. The Protestant minister who heads the Interfaith Conference explained, as the printed program indicated, "why we are here." Next, music from the Baha'i community, followed by a congregational song led by a guitar-playing rabbi. A female Episcopal priest led a guided "Meditation on Life."

Then there was a Sikh prayer, with drum and strings, led by a turbaned friend who introduced himself as Diane's dentist. A woman who founded the Martin Luther King Support Group read an excerpt from Dr. King's writings. A Jewish layperson read the "Prayer of St. Francis" to the rabbi's guitar accompaniment. Then the physician who heads the Neonatal Intensive Care Unit at Georgetown University Hospital shed his shoes and stood at the podium to offer a Hindu prayer. After the "passing of peace," the director of the Mormon Choir of Washington led the group in singing "How Great Thou Art."

Diane's sister and two nieces spoke about faith and family as Diane had experienced it growing up. Next, I read Romans 12:1–21. After that Diane spoke to the assembly from her wheelchair and from her heart. And then, to chanting and drumming in the spirit of Eastern religions, the group moved downstairs for a reception and table discussion about their religious similarities and differences. When it was all over, a Catholic woman, a Holy Trinity parishioner, said to me, "I've never been so convinced as I am right now that we are all praying to the same God."

As Cardinal Walter Kasper said that year in his Washington lecture to the Catholic Common Ground Initiative, "[I]nterreligious dialogue, especially the dialogue with Judaism, has become a defining characteristic of the life of the Church. In fact, since the Second Vatican Council dialogue has become a fundamental expression and feature of Catholicism." He added, "As human beings, we do not only carry on dialogue, we are dialogue."

Diane Sherwood gave a smiling amen to that in what proved to be the last September of her life. She was then and, I believe, still is dialogue. She was back at Trinity for Sunday masses that fall, sometimes with and sometimes without a wheelchair, but died a few months later.

Although we refer at times to someone as a "fixture" at a given Sunday liturgy, we know that all of us are passing through. No "fixture" is a permanent part of any worshipping community. Diane was there in her time showing us the way. Her faith then was fixed in eternity where she now lives. I and so many others were blessed that she decided in her last September to share that faith with those she loved and who will always love her in return.

15. Eugene McCarthy: Neat and Clean for Gene

Parting Shots from My Brittle Bow was former Minnesota Senator Eugene McCarthy's last book. I had it with me when I visited him in an assisted living facility in Washington, hoping to have him sign it. But he was bedridden at that time and the effort would have been a bit much.

He was eighty-nine when he died in 2005. As a member of the U.S. House of Representatives, the U.S. Senate, a candidate for the Democratic nomination for president in 1968, a professor, poet, social commentator, and an independent presidential candidate in 1976, McCarthy's place in history is secure. Although it was difficult to hear his words when I visited him toward the end, there was still a sparkle in the eye and a smile of remembrance at the mention of names and stories past.

Many of those who emerged from the ranks of the antiwar movement as "neat and clean for Gene" to pour their energies into his campaign that ended in disappointment at the Democratic Convention in Chicago in 1968 sent cards and letters and made occasional visits to the retirement residence in Washington, DC, where he ended his days.

"The bow is pretty brittle now," he remarked when I

mentioned the book. But the shots, I want to say for the record, were still very much on the mark.

An admirer, Sam Scinta, edited McCarthy's last book, *Parting Shots*. He recalled early in 2004 reading an interview with the Senator in the *New Yorker* where McCarthy said that the *New York Times* and *Washington Post* were no longer interested in his views on politics. "I was shocked," wrote Scinta, in the introduction to *Parting Shots*, "that a figure of such intellect and insight was being 'put out to pasture' by the major news organizations." So Scinta immediately wrote to the man he had long admired, offered his services as an editor ready to gather up past speeches, interviews, and previously unpublished material for a new book. The subject was willing and the eight-chapter result bears the simple subtitle: "Reflections on American Politics and Life."

Eugene McCarthy's "basic premises" were our nation is shaped by a democratic principle that requires involvement on the part of both public officials and those who elect them; many of the institutions we need for a well-functioning democracy are in a state of disrepair; nonetheless, hope prevails; the two-party system is obsolete; and America has a unique role to play in world affairs.

The McCarthy humor was legendary:

> "You really have to be careful of politicians who have no further ambitions: they may run for the presidency."

> "If a man was drowning twenty feet from shore, a Republican would throw him a fifteen-foot rope and say, 'Well, I went more than half way.'"

"Being a successful politician is like being a successful football coach. You have to be smart enough to understand the game, and dumb enough to think it's important."

McCarthy had lots of wisdom as well:

"There is no place in the world today and no person in the world for which we do not have some degree of obligation and responsibility."

"It is the inequality of a burden, not its weight, which usually provokes resistance."

"Knowledge and reason, limited though they may be, are the only defenses of civilization against ignorance and false fear. Together or apart, they give stability and direction to civilization."

In a poem titled "Gene," Samuel Hazo wrote: "Almost unannounced, you landed/in New Hampshire, spoke/to smallish but determined crowds/and entered history." And in his 1998 "Lament of an Aging Politician," McCarthy gave a poet's reply: "I have left Act I, for involution/and Act II. There mired in/complexity/I cannot write Act III."

Close to a thousand gathered for a memorial service in the Washington National Cathedral on the Saturday morning of Presidents' Day weekend 2005. Former President Bill Clinton gave a eulogy recalling how he, as a recent graduate of Georgetown holding a nondescript internship on Capitol Hill, received, through the intervention of an influential elder in whose home Clinton happened to be staying, an invitation to a black-tie dinner at the White House. "I can rent a tux," said the young Clinton to his host, "but I don't own a pair of black shoes." "I'll ask my neighbor to lend you a pair," said his mentor.

Within minutes the neighbor was there on the front porch with a pair of black shoes in hand. Clinton recognized the lender to be none other than Eugene McCarthy, who, Clinton recalled, sat on the porch and chatted with the young Democrat from Arkansas for about a half hour.

"When I got to the White House that night," said the future president, "I took a look at the reception line and said to myself, 'I can't walk up and shake hands with President Nixon while wearing Gene McCarthy's shoes.'" As the laughter subsided, Bill Clinton added: "And I'm just one of many who have been walking in Gene McCarthy's shoes ever since."

16. Rene D'Agostino: Special Delivery

This story could possibly have come from the U.S. Postal Service, Fed Ex, or any one of a large number of organizations that deliver greetings and packages at Christmastime. It happens to come from United Parcel Service (UPS), the company that runs those big, boxy, brown trucks on highways and streets all over the country and around the world. This is a Christmas story about a UPS driver, Rene D'Agostino, making her routine rounds just a day or two before Christmas on a military base known as the Aberdeen Proving Ground in Maryland.

Michael Eskew, chairman and CEO of UPS, tells the story with pride. The base was fairly empty on that day, he said, because most of the military personnel were on Christmas leave. Rene D'Agostino found herself trying to deliver an overnight letter with no specific address, just a name on the envelope. She asked a few people on that sprawling base if they recognized the name; no one did.

Then, Eskew explained, the driver called her UPS supervisor to ask if she could open the envelope to look for some clue as to the recipient's whereabouts. All she found inside was a money order and a handwritten note: "Make me happy. Come home for Christmas. Love, Mom."

The driver figured it out. The money order was there to pay for the soldier's trip home. But where was he? She drove to the on-base house of a Marine officer. He didn't recognize the name but agreed to open his office and run a computer search. Sure enough, he located the Marine and identified his barracks. So, accompanied by a Sergeant-at-Arms, the UPS driver entered the barracks, but her man wasn't there. One of his buddies said he had gone to the rec center on base. Off went Rene to find him. He was there, sitting on a couch, surrounded by a stack of rented movies. Apparently, a movie marathon was going to get him through a lonely Christmas.

"I've got something for you," said Rene, and handed him the opened envelope. He read the note, smiled, sprang off the couch, hugged the driver, and started for the door when he remembered the videos. He turned back to Rene and asked her for one more favor—could she drop those movies off at the rec center rental counter for him? She delivered.

All of us are delivering all sorts of things to all sorts of people all of the time. Not so dramatic as this UPS delivery, perhaps, but we deliver. Sometimes it is just a smile or a word of greeting.

Each of us is a link in a chain. Christmas is a time to think of the connections, even passing connections we make with one another. Thank God for the Rene D'Agostinos of the world who, in meeting their ordinary workplace responsibilities, use some imagination and expend some extra effort to make the kind of connections that make Christmas the warm and wonderful experience it should be for everyone.

17. Geno Baroni: The Wisdom of Ordinary People

It is hard to believe so many years have passed since the death, from cancer, at age fifty-three, of Monsignor Geno Baroni on August 27, 1984. It is even harder to have to acknowledge that, for the most part, American Catholics have forgotten who he was.

We cannot afford to forget Geno Baroni. He was a Washington, DC, priest and civil-rights activist in the 1960s; an ethnic neighborhood organizer in the '70s; and, after advising candidate Jimmy Carter in the presidential campaign of 1976, an Assistant Secretary of Housing and Urban Development in the Carter Administration.

Geno Baroni had deep confidence in the wisdom of ordinary people. He valued institutions but worked to hold them accountable, accessible, and responsive to ordinary people. He always looked for ways to establish linkages, to form connections. He thought public policy should be "good news" for the poor. In the Baroni perspective, "policy is people." His aim was to make the personal political; he would move from home, to neighborhood, to City Hall, and on up the line. The neighborhood- or community-organizer's task is to help people "politicize" their own good instincts. In addition, Baroni awakened in the hearts of countless talented and generous people a response, translated into career commitments, to the imperative of working for social justice.

Baroni was a complicated genius who did things viscerally, not intellectually. He was not a linear thinker. He moved in patterns rather than in straight lines. He worked the phones, not the typewriter. He had really only one speech; it personalized and interpreted what was known in the 1970s as the "white ethnic movement." The basic speech was never written down until after his death when Larry O'Rourke produced his 1991 book *Geno* and in it reconstructed "The Speech" in a chapter titled, "Geno's Parables."

I've often wished that we had some Baroni Centers around the country that would train social activists in the Baroni method shaped by what I like to think of as the Baroni principles. If that day ever comes, here are some of Geno's principles that will find their way into the curriculum:

The role of the Church in social action is to help convene people.

The organizer has to get ordinary people in touch with their roots, their heritage, their best.

The organizer has to have deep respect for the ordinary in ordinary people.

The organizer has to give ordinary people hope.

The way to break down walls is to go around them by building bridges, forming coalitions, forging bonds.

Work from idea, to committee, to coalition.

If you want to save the city, and the country, and the world, you have to start in the neighborhood where people live.

Neighborhood survival means parish survival; parish survival means neighborhood survival.

Apathy and violence are cousins coming from the same font—despair. When there is no way out—lack of opportunity, growing frustration, and despair—there is a new kind of psychological poverty that leads to continued apathy and despair.

Values are at the core of any organizing effort. Respond to people's deepest hopes and aspirations.

Never rent a hall you can't fill.

It is easier to obtain forgiveness than to get permission.

When you make a mistake, admit it; then pick up the pieces and move on.

Today's troubled American Church would do well to incorporate a few Baroni principles into its renewal and repair strategies. As Geno used to say, "Action follows teaching by way of experience."

18. Weltha Wentling: Anonymity Has Its Own Rewards

It is sometimes remarked that behind every successful man you will find a surprised mother-in-law. Let the reader make his or, more important, her own judgment about the accuracy of that statement. There is, however, no surprise and no dispute that behind most notable achievers is a seldom-noticed teacher.

At the Greater Washington Board of Trade's "2002 Leader of the Year" award dinner, I heard a very successful man pay a moving tribute to his third-grade teacher. In his acceptance speech, John P. McDaniel, CEO of MedStar Health, told a gathering of movers and shakers in the national capital's business community, "When I was in third grade in Carey, Ohio, my teacher was Weltha Wentling, a kindly, dedicated lady who never married and whose whole life was teaching."

Why mention her on that occasion? Because, as a child, McDaniel said, he struggled with an unidentified problem that we now know as dyslexia. "She kept me after school every afternoon," said the honoree, "working with me, teaching me how to read. I remember her saying, 'John, we're going to figure this reading thing out.' And we did."

"I didn't know it then, and wasn't even very grateful at the time," said John McDaniel, "but Weltha Wentling changed my life. Weltha Wentling, who reached out to a floundering young student, was a leader in the truest sense of the word."

MedStar Health is a not-for-profit health care organization integrating thirty hospitals and health care organizations in the Washington-Baltimore region. It is the fifth largest employer in the region with twenty-two thousand on the payroll and over four thousand affiliated physicians, serving more than a half-million patients each year. It takes a lot of reading to be able to lead an organization like this. It took a lot of patience back in Carey, Ohio, to teach this future executive how first to read in order later to lead.

"Sister Genevieve was my sixth-grade teacher at St. Mathieu's School in Fall River, Massachusetts," said syndicated political columnist and social justice advocate E. J. Dionne, Jr. in reply to David Shribman's inquiry about most memorable teachers. "She got kicked out of the South in the 1960s because she organized a biracial communion service. She was no radical, but she taught me more than anyone else about racial justice without saying much of anything." David Shribman's book, *I Remember My Teacher*, was published by Andrews McMeel.

Walter Sheridan's career as an investigator began after graduation from Fordham in 1949. He went from the National Security Agency, to the FBI, on to close collaboration with Robert F. Kennedy in the 1950s on a Senate committee investigating corruption in organized labor. When Kennedy became attorney general, Sheridan went with him to the Justice Department as a special assistant charged with the task of exposing corruption in the Teamsters Union. And when Kennedy went to the Senate, Sheridan, who once told me that the person who had the greatest influence on his life was the nun who taught him in the fifth grade in Utica, New York, became an investigative reporter for NBC News.

"In Defense of Honest Labor" was the way the *New York Times Magazine* summed up the career of Walter Sheridan after his death in 1995. That unnamed nun in Utica never knew that she would have anything to do with a career of a man who, as the *Times* put it, tried "to save the labor movement from the enemy within," and "help thousands of people who would never know his name."

Anonymity has its own rewards!

PART THREE
Spirituality

19. Thinking about Hope

It seems to me that hope is a seldom-used tool in the Catholic tool kit.

So it was more than timely for Pope Benedict XVI to issue an encyclical early in his pontificate that took its opening sentence from St. Paul's Letter to the Romans (8:24): "*Spe salvi facti sumus*"—"in hope we were saved."

I'm puzzled at the way the word *hopefully* worked its misapplied way into our American vernacular. That adverb means "in a happily expectant way." Like *cheerfully*, it conveys a mood. Hope is substance; hopefulness is style. *Hopefully* suggests a bounce in your walk, some lilt in your voice.

Are you really full of hope and happily expectant when you say "hopefully"? Or are you struggling with doubt and trying to sound brave? Instead of saying "hopefully," you should probably be saying—from the depths of my doubt or uncertainty—"It is to be hoped" that this or that outcome will emerge.

Hope is an engine to drive your dreams into the unknown future.

Just as sorrow can make you sorrowful, hope can make you hopeful. From the inside, this mood feels good. From the outside it is typically seen as something light, bright, and cheery, although it can work just as well under cover of seriousness. Hope is an anchor that connects you securely to God.

There is a wonderful book called *Images of Hope* written back in 1965 by a Jesuit priest by the name of William Lynch. He was a genuine Christian humanist. He points, in the best humanistic tradition, to "imagination as healer of the hopeless." Lynch saw hope as "the very heart and center of a human being." And he says that hope must be tied to the life of the imagination. I'll let Father Lynch speak for himself.

> I define hope...as the fundamental knowledge and feeling that there is a way out of difficulty, that things can work out, that we as human persons can somehow handle and manage internal and external reality, that there are "solutions" in the most ordinary biological and physiological sense of that word, that, above all, there are ways out of illness.
>
> What [I'm] saying is that hope is, in its most general terms, a sense of the possible, that what we really need is possible, though difficult, while hopelessness means to be ruled by the sense of the impossible. Hope therefore involves three basic ideas that could not be simpler: what I hope for I do not yet have or see; it may be difficult; but I can have it—it is possible.
>
> Hope looks to the next step, whatever it is, whatever form the step may take. If there is hope, I take [the step]. We are too much inclined to think of hope as an emergency virtue that saves itself for a crisis (one that is really meant for use in moments when there is not much or any hope at all!). The truth is that [hope] is present in each

moment as it looks to the next. [Hope] is present everywhere, in the flowing of the bloodstream and in every small action. I would not breathe if I did not hope that the air around me would respond to my call. (*Images of Hope*, pp. 24–25)

The words of Psalm 27 would have us "Wait for the Lord, take courage, be stouthearted, and wait for the Lord." We are a waiting, wishing, hopeful people, who, precisely because we live by hope, step out to meet the demands of the present day as we make our way into an unknown future.

Hope can show you the way.

20. The Color of Hope Is Springtime Green

Mary Flynn was a popular professor of social work at The Catholic University of America. First and foremost, she was a wonderful wife and mother. Mary arranged her teaching schedule so that she could be home at lunchtime with and for her children, whose elementary school was just a couple of blocks distant from their home.

When Mary died, her adult children held a wake service for her at home. Hundreds of friends passed through the house to offer condolences and express both sympathy and love. A homemade prayer service included reflections and remembrances from the children Mary left behind.

One daughter recalled a troubled moment in her twelve-year-old life when she found herself at home with her mother on a bitterly cold winter day as the body of the mother of her best friend lay "somewhere" in a casket, as yet unburied, because the frozen ground could not be opened for a grave. "Promise me you won't die in winter," the daughter recalled saying to her mother. "When will you die, Mom, do you know?"

And Mary Flynn, without answering, simply walked over to the phonograph, selected a record from the rack, put it on the turntable, and returned to sit beside her daughter and hug her as they listened to the voice of Robert Goulet singing, "If Ever I Would Leave You." The lyrics moved melodically through the four seasons, providing a memorable background for the reassurance a mother's embrace was able to give to an anxious child who was comforted to hear that "it would never be in springtime."

But it is springtime once every year. In any springtime there may be war and illness; there will surely be death. We always need hope.

"Younger Than Springtime," another old favorite, carries a message that may or may not match up with the date on your birth certificate. But anyone can be young at heart and smiling in springtime. We may have very good reason to be sad, but springtime wants us to pack away that sadness with our winter clothes.

Spring fever? There is probably a medical basis for that expression somewhere in the pediatric literature, but the implied slowdown has to yield to the ubiquitous evidence of a spring-in-the-step and a smile on the face. If fever it be, let it be an elevated expectancy for better days ahead.

"The flowers of spring"? That familiar phrase says, or better, sings it all, doesn't it? Weeks earlier there were just buried bulbs and barren branches; now look at the display of life. And you, with a springtime smile, are indeed "as welcome as the flowers of spring" to dear old wherever you call home.

Some think of spring cleaning; others of spring break. Everyone thinks green, not as the color of money, but the color of hope. The greening of the spirit is part of any spring-time cleaning up and breaking away. *Wheat That Springeth Green* is not simply the title of a novel, it is nature's reminder that everything needed to sustain both life and hope is now surrounding you.

Life, as we know it on this beautiful earth, cannot last forever. We acknowledge that with a touch of sadness, per-haps, but with our faith firmly planted and, by virtue of our faith, we stand prepared.

Those in the "eldering" ranks are grateful to be able to elder their way with measured steps into another springtime in any given year. The youngsters, God bless them, take carefree hops, skips, and jumps into their unknown future. Whether you are eldering out or jumping in, or somewhere in between, you have plenty of reason for hope as the greening begins around you every year and gratitude wells up from within.

21. Strength Is Virtue and Virtue Is Strength

When you were a child did you ever invite an elder to "feel my muscle"? Little boys and girls alike, but mostly boys, will extend an arm, clench a fist, bend an elbow, and stare at the slightest hint of a bulging bicep in the upper arm. "See how strong I am!"

Boys at play (perhaps girls as well; I don't know) like to adopt "strong" names. "Call me Steve," was a familiar request in my own childhood circle of friends that included no one named Stephen. "Bobby," "Billy," or "George" just wouldn't do it. Neither would "Jimmy," even in those days of tough-guy Jimmy Cagney movies where the hoodlum was the hero and the cops often objects of ridicule.

"Let me carry him" (usually a younger brother). "I can lift it" (often a piece of porch furniture). We can all recall our participation in claims or demonstrations of physical strength in those tender years before we ever heard of hernias. The strength myth (strong man, strong woman, strong arm, strong will, strong statement, strong medicine) persists to the point of locking our minds and emotions into some kind of "strong box" to which we have lost the key that will open us up to tears, admission of error or defeat, and an open declaration that we stand in need of help. This is a spiritual problem that needs attention.

"Bravery" is sometimes prideful ignorance, and ignorance can leave one "blissfully unaware" of where the real dangers lurk. Strength is virtue and virtue is strength. The virtuous person will become strongest in the broken places.

The season of summer fun and games is a good time to think seriously about teaching our kids the real meaning of strength, especially the relationship of strength to virtue. All of us, young or old, need to be reminded that we can, by God's grace, become strong in our broken places.

Job loss, health setbacks, marital stress, geopolitical problems, and personal tensions large or small can drain anyone's strength. I can still hear my exasperated mother saying "God, give me strength!" in reaction to the summertime carelessness of her offspring, who hit baseballs through garage-door windows and, on one otherwise unchallenging summer day, dug a large hole behind our house in the first stage of a children's tunnel project intended to connect

Philadelphia with Peking. Perhaps we should make "God, give me strength" a national prayer in these days [2009] of frozen credit markets, stock market turbulence, soaring gasoline prices, plummeting real estate values, rising unemployment rates, urban crime, highway mishaps, and a lengthening list of societal problems.

Many of these problems are likely to get worse over the next few decades. Those who will then be in the driver's seat of any vehicle designed to move us toward social progress are the very youngsters who enjoy their fun and freedom in the summertime. They need adult encouragement in that developmental time of their life to understand that real strength is strength of character and that qualities like creativity, courage, and intellectual competence are the "muscles" most in need of development.

22. Entitlement and Ingratitude

The weeks between Thanksgiving and Christmas provide me with an annual context for reflection on an important religious question—the relationship of entitlement to ingratitude.

Thanksgiving, of course, puts the accent where it should be—on giving, saying, and doing thanks. Men and women of faith target God first and foremost for expressions of gratitude on Thanksgiving Day. Even nonbelievers, I suspect, welcome this American invention of a secular feast day for the occasion it provides to look left and right, if not up to heaven, to say thanks for benefits, if not blessings; and for good luck, if not the generosity of the Good Lord.

Once in the thanks-saying, thanks-giving, thanks-doing mood of late November, it is quite literally a short step to

Christmas, which, one might expect, should be a season of great gratitude. However, I've noticed at Christmastime and in other seasons of the year, a rising sense of entitlement in America, especially among the young. I've begun to conclude that ingratitude is the infrastructure of entitlement.

Ignatius of Loyola once remarked that "ingratitude is at the root of all sinfulness." He was on to something. When ingratitude takes over one's outlook, there is an erosion of a sense of obligation, including moral obligation. "Much obliged" is a way the old American vernacular had of saying thanks. If you have nothing to be thankful for—that is, if you consider yourself to be entitled to everything you have and might receive—you are unencumbered by a sense of any obligation. You are free to be your selfish, solipsistic, narcissistic self.

Total self-absorption is another word for sin.

A decade or more ago I found myself describing students I was then meeting in the college classroom as characterized by a sense of entitlement. They "deserved" good grades, good health, good jobs, and the best of everything the world had to offer. Cultural reinforcement for this attitude of entitlement came, and continues to come, through their entertainment and advertising, their words and music, their images and apparel. There are cures for all their ills, solutions for all their problems, answers (with or without the help of a search engine) to all their questions. It is all within reach. It is theirs for the taking. No need to say thanks.

This outlook has seeped down into high school and middle school minds—to the teens and tweens who never say thanks.

So, what did you get for Christmas? Now that you've got it, are you happier than before? Are you disappointed that it wasn't what you really wanted or, worse, that it is not as good as something someone you know has received? Many years ago I pressed a child for a working definition of the word *gift*. "A gift is when somebody gives you something," she said. I responded, "What if I had borrowed a dollar from you earlier and now I'm giving it back. Here, take the dollar. Is that a gift? It fits your definition."

A moment's pondering prompted the youngster to revise her definition and say, "A gift is when you get something you don't deserve."

How true. How very appropriate for Christmas reflection. What a positive indicator that we have, through an awareness of gratitude, a way of protecting ourselves from the virus of entitlement. Each year Christmas will be a good deal merrier and happier for all if we realize that the gifts we exchange are not only undeserved, but symbols to remind us that Christmas is a worldwide celebration of the gift of salvation to which none of us has a claim, except through our faith in Christ Jesus the Lord.

23. Substance Abuse, Religion, and Spirituality

"So Help Me God" is the title of a "white paper" released a few years ago by the National Center on Addiction and Substance Abuse (CASA) at Columbia University. The paper's subtitle is: "Substance Abuse, Religion, and Spirituality."

CASA chairman and president, Joseph A. Califano, Jr., held a press conference at the National Press Club in

Washington, DC, to release the report and announce the key finding of this two-year study, namely, that religion and spirituality should be in harness with "the power of science and professional medicine to prevent and treat substance abuse and addiction."

If the clergy knew more about addiction to drugs and alcohol, and if psychiatrists and psychologists understood how religion and spirituality can contribute to prevention and cure of these diseases, millions of Americans would benefit. But there are two "disconnects" that must first be overcome. The first is that clergy know next to nothing about the causes and medical responses to the problem. And the second is the failure of the medical profession to appreciate the role of religion and spirituality in treating substance abusers and addicts.

Of the clergy CASA surveyed for this study, only 12.5 percent had any coursework related to these problems in the seminary, and only 36.5 percent preach about the issue more than once a year. The study also found that only 45 percent of mental health practitioners report a belief in God and thus don't even think about the possibility that spiritual interventions could contribute to patient progress.

An authoritative *Source Book of Substance Abuse and Addiction*, aimed at "curing physicians of their unfortunate 'blind spot' about drug abuse and addiction," emerged from the Harvard Medical School in 1996. I consulted it after reading the CASA report and searched in vain for any reference to religion or spirituality anywhere in the book. Despite (or better because of) this deficit, the book belongs in the hands of ministers of religion. What reading might they want to recommend to cure physicians of their "blind spot" relative to the preventive and curative potential of religion in the battle with addiction? The Book of Psalms would be good for openers.

Sprinkled throughout the CASA report are data to support the claim that adults who consider religion to be important and practice their faith are far less likely to use illicit drugs and abuse alcohol than are those who disregard religion. "Teens who never attend religious services are twice as likely to drink, more than three times likelier to use marijuana and binge drink, and almost four times likelier to use illicit drugs than teens who attend religious services at least weekly," according to the study.

The CASA study calls for action on three fronts:

> Priests, ministers, rabbis, and imams "should become more engaged in addressing this problem, formally preaching about substance abuse issues and incorporating prevention and recovery messages in their ministry."

> Physicians and treatment providers "should be better trained and informed of the importance of spirituality and religion to prevention and treatment... and of the spiritual and religious resources available in their local communities."

> More research is needed "to better understand and enhance the complementary roles that religion and professional substance abuse treatment can play in prevention, treatment and recovery."

It is late, but certainly not too late, for health care providers and ministers of religion to begin appreciating more and reinforcing what each can do to help sick people break the shackles of addiction.

24. Pain Relief and the Spirit of Suffering

I served for a while on the board of directors of the now defunct Last Acts Partnership, a Washington-based, not-for-profit advocacy group interested in promoting quality end-of-life care.

Last Acts participated with the federal Drug Enforcement Administration and the Pain and Policy Studies Group at the University of Wisconsin in the production of a document titled "Prescription Pain Medications: Frequently Asked Questions and Answers for Health Care Professionals and Law Enforcement Personnel."

This publication, available in print from DEA, is also available online without charge at www.usdoj.gov/dea and www.stoppain.org. It is intended to improve patient care by offering guidance on the appropriate uses of prescription pain medication at any time, not just as the end of life draws near.

Balance and *prudence* are the words that come to mind the more I learn about the question of prescribing potentially addictive medications to ease pain. All interested parties, including law enforcement, must be prudent; hence the importance of clear information and informed guidelines.

There are, as we all know, risks of abuse—that is, risks of illegal use and criminal diversion of pain-relief drugs by both patients and providers. There is also the risk that is a major concern for providers, namely, the unintended consequence of addiction. Prudence simply has to be a permanent partner, a constant guide of those committed to caring for patients in pain at any stage in life.

Patients have a right not to suffer pain when the reduction or elimination of pain is medically possible. Last Acts got into this act, so to speak, in developing this report because of its mission to ease pain endured by patients as life on this earth is drawing to a close.

Interest in the report, however, is more intense among providers who fear running afoul of the law in prescribing pain relief for patients who are not terminal, and among law-enforcement officers who want to be compassionate, but also realistic, in the face of possible abuse.

There is, in the best sense of the word, an end-of-life *constituency* in the United States. It is solid, right intentioned, far from any fringe, but small. The general public needs better information. The provider community—hospitals, pharmacists, nurses, and physicians—wants clarity. Law enforcement at all levels has a lot of questions. This publication provides the answers to those frequently asked questions.

An opiate is a substance produced from the poppy plant, such as codeine and morphine. An opioid is a natural or synthetic drug that affects the central and peripheral nervous systems. Most patients on long-term opioid therapy develop physical dependence.

A basic premise of this report reads: "As the U.S. population ages, people will live longer with chronic, often painful diseases. Even if opioids are appropriate for only a small proportion of these patients, nothing should be done to limit access to the drugs when they are needed or to increase the reluctance of prescribers to recommend them."

Christian theology and spirituality respect the redemptive power of human pain accepted and willingly joined to the sufferings of Christ for the salvation of the world. Also respected is the patient's right not to suffer what medical and pharmaceutical intervention can prevent. There is a need in this contemporary discussion to hear the voice of Christian tradition and to attend to what it has been saying for centuries about the redemptive power of human suffering.

Balance of many interests, not least among them the interest of patients, their families, and their caregivers in easing, even eliminating pain, is the goal of the end-of-life constituency. This document helps most interests—all except the spiritual—to be heard in the struggle to achieve that goal with peace of mind. An opening to faith-based reflection on the theological significance of human suffering will elevate the debate and advance this worthy cause.

25. Workplace Spirituality

Labor Day announces the arrival of the Get Serious season. The self-improvement impulse strikes with varying degrees of intensity throughout the year, as we all know. It produces New Year's resolutions, summer reading lists, Advent and Lenten practices, and periodic diet plans. Labor Day marks the end of the lazy days of summer and starts the self-improvement ball bouncing once again.

Some say the spirit is willing but the flesh is weak. Well, if the spirit needs a bit of shoring up, Labor Day offers the opportunity for both business and labor to explore the possibility of finding spirituality in the workplace.

Those who habitually postpone self-improvement and

those whose feet are set in spirit-resistant cement would admire, if they took the time to notice, an age-old package of nine spiritual principles suited for the workplace. The reason, I suspect, why these nine virtues so often fail to become adopted as workplace-enhancing characteristics is that they are all too casually dismissed as "religious" and thus irrelevant to everyday workplace life.

But who among the most secular of persons would not like to possess and experience the following characteristics where they work: love, joy, peace, patience, kindness, generosity, faithfulness, gentleness, and self-control? These qualities are what St. Paul identifies in Galatians 5:23 as the "fruit" of the Spirit, evidence that the Holy Spirit is present within a human person. Paul wanted his Galatian friends, recent converts from paganism, to have guidelines for a free and balanced life—for maintaining the right balance between matter and spirit—in their worldly pursuits.

Now, 2000 years after Paul wrote to the Galatians, there is an emerging interest in America in workplace spirituality. Militating against this interest, however, is an unexamined presupposition on the part of the skeptical that the worlds of faith and work are irreparably split, that the spiritual life and the working life are quite literally worlds apart.

The most dynamic, assertive, and competitive human being can remain human and even prosper in the workplace by clothing his or her competitive assertiveness in the armor of love, joy, peace, patience, kindness, generosity, faithfulness, gentleness, and self-control. To say this cannot be so is to concede that there is no place for the Spirit of God in the material world created by God. These nine Pauline principles deserve, indeed demand attention in our day. What have we and our workplace world come to, if there is no room within either for the Creator of both?

Perhaps the problem lies in fundamental misconceptions about each of these nine realities. Contrary to what popular culture would have you believe, love is service and sacrifice. Joy is balance at the center of the soul. Peace is good order. Patience is the ability to endure whatever comes. Kindness is attentive regard for the other. Generosity is the habitual disposition to share. Faithfulness is a promise kept. Gentleness is courageous respect for others. Self-control is a voluntary check on the appetite for excess.

Once assimilated, these values become contagious. They transform persons and persons thus transformed can change the workplace without preaching, proselytizing, or arguing— just by being their transformed selves.

26. Sunday into Monday and Back Again

Ed Willock, editor of the now defunct Catholic monthly *Integrity*, seemed many years ago to delight in jogging the consciences of readers from the world of business with verse-barbs such as the following: "Mr. Business went to Mass; he never missed a Sunday. But Mr. Business went to hell for what he did on Monday!"

That dart still draws a chuckle, as it did when I included it in a talk in Phoenix, Arizona, at St. Francis Xavier Church where parishioners wanted to reflect on the relevance of religious faith to their weekday business and professional responsibilities. "Sunday into Monday" was the theme of a two-day parish retreat following preaching on that theme at all the Sunday masses.

Whether it hits as a dart or a harpoon, the Willock barb is wide of the mark in this era with its rising sense among Catholics of a vocation to business. But it is right on target as we continue to read press reports of bid-rigging, price-fixing, and undisclosed payments to brokers in the insurance industry, not to mention the problems of Enron, WorldCom, Arthur Andersen, and so many others who made the business ethics hit parade not all that long ago.

What is the relevance of religious faith to the workaday world? This is a question for all believers, not just Catholics.

Rabbi Abraham Joshua Heschel remarked many years ago that the problem for contemporary believers is not to figure out "how to worship in the catacombs, but how to remain human in the skyscrapers." And as I've indicated in the preceding essay, the qualities needed for that are the same values listed by St. Paul in his Letter to the Galatians (5:22–23), in which he told newcomers to the faith that the evidence or "fruit" of the Holy Spirit's presence in themselves and their communities (workplaces included) was this set of nine virtues: "love, joy, peace, patience, kindness, generosity, faithfulness, gentleness, and self-control."

In opposition to these, Paul listed "works of the flesh" —evidence of opposition to and absence of the Spirit. Included in this list of negatives (Gal 5:19–21) are a few familiar workplace issues, namely, "hatreds, rivalry, jealousy, outbursts of fury, acts of selfishness, dissensions, factions, occasions of envy," and the like.

So the Sunday challenge for worshipers is to internalize

the positive (and fully human) Pauline values that can be carried over into the workplace on Monday morning.

Eucharistic communities gather on Sunday to "remember the Lord in the breaking of the bread." They approach the altar "with bread" (the Latin words are *cum pane*). In expressing their praise and thanks to God, worshipers experience a companionship with one another. How to carry that companionship back to "the company," to the Monday-morning workplace, is another way of inquiring about the relevance of religious faith to business practice.

It helps if one thinks of oneself as "called" by God to whatever he or she does "for a living" during the week. It also helps if you imagine the Offertory procession beginning on Monday morning and moving day by day through the week, picking up along the way gifts from God—"fruit of the earth and the work of human hands"—to be offered back to God in grateful praise with the bread and wine presented at the altar on Sunday.

From that altar, you take the nourishment you need to carry the "fruit of the Spirit" back into the workplace or to other settings where, by God's grace, you spend your weekday life in fidelity to the vocation that is yours.

27. Social Love

Do you remember our Y2K anxiety as we approached the Year 2000? Where did it originate?

Some can still remember the old IBM punch cards. Decades ago someone came up with a clever way to "enlarge capacity" on those punch cards. They had eighty columns. You could gain column space by simply dropping the first two digits of the four-digit numeric designation for any calendar year. This gave no thought to the mess we would be in when computerized data would turn the corner from 1999 into the twenty-first century and click our records back to the year 1900 instead of into the year 2000.

We worried whether, after the stroke of midnight on December 31, 1999, airplanes and public utilities would be able to operate. Frenzied programmers and lots of money rescued us from that potential catastrophe.

Are you wondering who or what will come to our rescue next time? Some of us have no idea of what the next catastrophe might be, but we still worry!

In 1996, the bishops of England and Wales issued a pastoral warning to "beware of the tendency...to look to the future not for solutions but for more problems...[and] to fail to see that the nation's real crisis is not economic, but moral and spiritual." Surveys and studies of the national mood, wrote the bishops, "display a nation ill at ease with itself. Such surveys tell us that the British do not look forward to their society becoming fairer or more peaceful....They seem to be losing faith in the possibility of a better future."

The bishops saw the United Kingdom "being increasingly dominated by impersonal economic forces which leave little room for morality." They reminded their people of Pope John Paul II's repeated insistence that our human task "consists in the priority of ethics over technology, in the primacy of person over things, and the superiority of spirit over matter." But, the bishops found themselves forced to confess, "We believe that it is in the growing priority of technology over ethics, in the growing primacy of things over persons, and in the growing superiority of matter over spirit, that the most serious threats to British society now lie."

The same threats face us Americans as we worry whether security and peace will be ours.

The eye of Pope John Paul II looked to the coming of the twenty-first century as he wrote *Redemptor Hominis* in 1979. To reinforce their point, the British bishops quote from this encyclical: "If therefore our time, the time of our generation, the time that is approaching the end of the second millennium of the Christian era, shows itself to be a time of great progress, it is also seen as a time of threat to humanity in many forms. The Church must speak of this threat to all people of goodwill and must always carry on dialogue with them about it. Humanity's situation in the modern world seems indeed to be far removed from the objective demands of the moral order, from the requirements of justice, and even more of social love" (no. 16).

What is "social love"? What might one person do to help bring it about?

Alone, or in the family, it would be good to sketch out a description of "social love" as we are still in the early years of this new millennium. Here's a prayer of Teilhard de Chardin that can serve to get this reflection moving:

> Jesus, Savior of human activity to which you have given meaning, Savior of human suffering to which you have given value, be also the Savior of human unity; compel us to discard our pettiness, and to venture forth, resting upon You, into the uncharted ocean of love.

Without faith and hope, that reflection is not likely to begin. If it does begin, however, the discovery of social love may be within our reach.

PART FOUR
Peace and Justice

28. Reasoned Argument on the Road to Peace

The tranquility of right order is a classic definition of peace. If all the islands of tranquility in human hearts throughout the world were quilted together into one human mosaic, you would be looking at a representation of world peace. How wild a dream might that be?

Corwin Edwards once noted, "Brotherhood is not so wild a dream as those who profit by postponing it pretend." National and personal arrogance, greed, injustice, and mistrust postpone, to the point of prevention, the arrival of peace.

In the United States, it strains credulity for us to say, "In God We Trust," when our actions show that we prefer to put our trust in money, nuclear weapons, and unbreakable bolts on all our doors. As a Quaker and a pacifist, the late Steve Cary, retired vice president of Haverford College and long-time associate of the American Friends Service Committee, wrote a "Response to September Eleventh" in *Friends Journal* (March 2002), explaining his dissent from the view that we should wage a war on terrorism by taking a first strike at Iraq. His words are worth considering as we still quest for peace: "I think we should be troubled when we glance at our current budget: $340 billion for the power to kill; $6 billion for the power to lift the quality of life of the poor and dispossessed, on whose succor peace ultimately depends." If there is no relief of poverty, there will be no peace is the point he is making.

"Throughout history," Cary argues, "great powers and empires have always been tempted to go it alone, to pursue their own interests without regard for the interests of others. England was the victim of this mindset throughout the nineteenth century. In the twenty-first, are the immense wealth and power of the United States taking us down this road?" He saw evidence that we were taking that route in the attitude of the United States toward the United Nations in recent years (not meeting our dues commitments, turning to the United Nations only when it suits our purposes). Additional evidence is our withdrawal from the Anti-Ballistic Missile Treaty, and our reneging on other negotiated agreements like the Kyoto agreement on global warming and the Nuclear Test Ban Treaty.

Blasting Osama bin Laden and his lieutenants from their caves or killing them on the run will satisfy the widespread desire for vengeance, but "its price is too high and its contribution to easing the threat of terrorism too low," Cary said. There is a distinction between pacifism and nonviolence. An honest pacifist needs absolute assurance that violence is necessary when employed in pursuit of a lasting peace.

Prayer for peace should include prayer for those on either side of the argument as well as for those on both sides of the battle lines, however vaguely defined those lines might be.

We should also pray to preserve the peace whenever conflict threatens to erupt. There can be negotiated settlements of conflicting views and interests. Just because a fist is formed is no indication that a punch must be thrown. Conflict resolution is another term for peacemaking. John Courtney Murray used to like to quote Thomas Gilby's remark that "civilizations rest on men locked in argument." A good argument can contribute much to peace. Sound reasoning makes for good argument. Men and women "locked" in reasoned argument make peace possible.

That is worth remembering whenever political rhetoric separates itself from reasoned argument.

29. Give Peace a Prayer

There was an amazing interfaith gathering on the campus of Georgetown University when the 2006 International Prayer for Peace assembly brought to Washington, DC, from around the world representatives from most of the major religions.

It all started two decades earlier when Pope John Paul II thought it would be a good idea to invite to Assisi in Italy leaders of world religions to join their hands, hearts, and voices in prayer for peace. "Lord, make me an instrument of your peace," prayed the gentle Francis of Assisi back in the thirteenth century. Why not wake up the echo of that prayer in our own day and blend it in an international harmony of interfaith voices?

We talk about peace every day everywhere, and work for peace in diplomatic circles around the world, but only on special occasions do we assemble ecumenically in sacred space to pray for peace. In April 2006, the Archdiocese of Washington, DC, in cooperation with Georgetown University,

The Catholic University of America, and the Rome-based Sant' Egidio Community, hosted for the first time on American soil this two-day forum of interfaith discussion and peace prayer.

Remarkably, the event went unreported in the next day's *Washington Post*, although there was scattered and sporadic coverage in both the secular and religious media around the world. It would be wonderful if Americans could take a page from the statement that the ecumenical leaders, American and foreign, issued at the conclusion of their Washington gathering.

They referred to themselves as "men and women of different religions from the different continents of this world," and then explained that in assembling in America for the first time, they were "guided by the spiritual energy of the 'spirit of Assisi.'" "Here in Washington, DC," their statement read, "we have prayed, we have dialogued, and we have invoked God for the great gift of peace."

To the rest of the world they declared: "We want to say that those who use violence discredit their own cause. Those who believe that a greater violence is the response to the wrong they have suffered do not see the mountains of hatred they help create. Peace is the name of God. God never wants the elimination of the other; the sons and daughters of our adversaries are never our enemies: They are children to love and protect, all of them."

Signers of the statement see interfaith dialogue as "a medicine that heals wounds and helps make this world more livable for present and future generations." They urged us all "to have the courage to live the art of dialogue...[so] that the world may open to the hope of a new era of peace and justice."

A point raised in one of the many panel discussions during this assembly is that religious people tend to privatize forgiveness as a matter between one person and another, or between an individual and his or her God. They thus fail to see the potential for peace that lies in forgiveness of one nation by another, or in intercultural forgiveness as a route to the elimination of prejudice.

On days like the Fourth of July, when patriotism is literally paraded through the communities, large and small, of America, it is worth thinking about our readiness to forgive nations who may have wronged us, our tendency to surround our celebration of independence with the sights and sounds of violence, and our forgetfulness of praying ecumenically, openly, and publicly for the great gift of peace.

Forgiveness is the key to lasting peace.

30. Before Going to War Ask, "What Price Victory?"

On Saturday afternoons in the autumn, as the football scores are announced over the air, I'm intrigued by the "varsity verb." One team does not simply "defeat" another. Sportscasters use verbs like *trounce*, *thump*, *crush*, and *flatten* in tracing the path to victory: The varsity verb has only one target: *victory*.

In sports, politics, and war, in any contest at all, the object is victory. Former Minnesota Senator Eugene McCarthy's sardonic humor is still quoted in Washington gatherings: "Being a successful politician is like being a successful football coach," he often remarked. "You have to be smart enough to understand the game and dumb enough to think it's important." Not all would agree with that, of course, nor should they. Nor do most of us believe the sideline wisdom that, "Winning isn't the most important thing; it's the only thing!" The "only thing" that matters in sports, politics, or warfare, our better judgment tells us, is "how we play the game."

The word *victory* always reminds me of the cover story in *Time* magazine that reported the end of the Second World War. That August 20, 1945, issue came to my attention many years later. It's worth a trip to the library and a search of the microfilm records to read it now. Written without attribution of authorship (I later learned that a very young James Agee wrote the story), *Time*'s report appeared under a three-tiered headline. The overarching headline was "Victory." The first subhead was "The Peace," and the next subhead was "The Bomb."

Victory was not something simply to be celebrated back in 1945. It called for prayerful gratitude. It also called for prayerful pondering of the profound consequences of the use of the bomb that brought World War II to a sudden end. This victory thrust us into the Atomic Age, where the potential for both good and evil associated with the uses of atomic power bordered on the infinite. After mentioning the "splitting of the atom," *Time* made careful note of "this terrible split in the fact that upon a people already so nearly drowned in materialism even in peacetime, the good uses of this power might easily bring disaster as prodigious as the evil...."

We've been living with that worry since 1945.

All of our victories in sports, war, and politics have to be examined in light of a simple question: In what way did our gain come at the expense of another's loss? Is it fair or unfair gain that constitutes our victory? Were the winner's points won within the rules? Was the loser fairly defeated or unjustly cheated? Where is honor in this victory? We should be sure going in that the contest is right, and fair, and just.

That's why reflective Americans raised questions about Iraq. Pope John Paul II opposed that war. The citizens' lobby Common Cause asked: "Why now? Should we act alone? What are the consequences of a nuclear power taking pre-emptive, first-strike action against Iraq?"

In 1945, *Time* ended its victory story by observing, "Now reason and spirit meet on final ground. If either or anything is to survive, they must find a way to create an indissoluble partnership." Here we are these many years later still struggling to bring reason, which produced the bomb, and spirit, which must govern its use, together around the question of nuclear war.

Why can't we take that struggle more seriously?

31. Invoking Romero in Pursuit of Peace and Justice

On March 14, 2008, there was a lecture in Camden, New Jersey—the eighth annual—in a series honoring the memory of Archbishop Oscar Romero of El Salvador. It is sponsored each year by the Romero Center, a ministry of St. Joseph's Pro-Cathedral in Camden.

Why Camden? Because it is one of the poorest and most crime-ridden cities in the country. Why Romero? Because the Romero legacy is an expression of the Church's preferential option for the poor. The Romero Center fosters an understanding and application of what might be called

Romero principles to pressing urban social problems. The annual lecture is held on the Camden campus of Rutgers University, which is more than a convenient venue; without the application of the intellectual resources that a university has to offer, Camden's social problems will just get worse.

The lecture topic was "Faith and Politics: How Does Our Faith Inform Us as We Prepare for the November Elections?" If it is interesting to see a cathedral and a state university cooperating in this way, it is even more noteworthy, as the planners of the lecture intended, to acknowledge that the link between faith and politics needs exploration in order to find solutions to practical problems of urban crime and poverty.

There is, of course, in our country, a separation of Church and state that has to be respected, but there is no separation of Church and society. The Church—in this case the Camden Cathedral—has to be involved if the city is to become more receptive to the coming of the promised kingdom of God, which, as we all know, is to be a reign of justice, love, and peace. Lowering the barriers to the coming of the promised kingdom means reducing injustice, hatred, and all forms of violence. In facing up to this challenge, the people of God in Camden are quietly showing other local churches the way.

Past Romero lectures—all seven of them—are available in a small book titled *Romero's Legacy: The Call to Peace and Justice*, edited by Pilar Hogan Closkey and John P. Hogan, whose introduction to this book discusses "Romero's Vision and the City Parish—Urban Ministry and Urban Planning."

The pastor of St. Joseph's Pro-Cathedral, Father Robert T. McDermott, is a Camden native and vicar-general of the diocese. He is founder of the Romero Center. His chapter in this book puts the reader "In the Footsteps of Martyrs: Lessons from Central America." After making a pilgrimage to El Salvador he was able, he writes, "to grasp better and to radicalize the gospel in my own ministry and in our work here in Camden." He observes that "Archbishop Romero wanted the Church to be neither a museum piece nor a political organization. But he knew that to be the true continuation of the Incarnation, the Church had to take up the challenge of justice in all of its political, social, and economic dimensions."

No surprise then to find subsequent chapters highlighting "The Eucharist and Social Justice" (John P. Hogan), "If You Want Peace, Work for Justice" (Thomas J. Gumbleton), "Liberation Theology for the Twenty-First Century" (Gustavo Gutiérrez), and chapters on the death penalty by Sister Helen Prejean, on racism by Professor Diana Hayes, and on immigration by Daniel F. Groody.

This small book offers much to stimulate thought. Camden's poor are certainly hoping that it will stimulate action.

32. The Romero Prayer

This short reflection might fit more appropriately in either Part Three: Spirituality or Part Five: Church of this book, or Part Seven: Purpose, but I want to place it here as an extension of the preceding references to Archbishop Oscar Romero.

Whenever I read it in public, I'm always asked for printed copies. It's called the "Romero Prayer." El Salvadoran Archbishop Oscar Romero, who was killed by a government assassin's bullet while offering mass on March 24, 1980, probably never saw or heard it. He certainly didn't write it. But it provides such a perfect interpretative framework for a courageous life that met apparent defeat in a violent death, that admirers of the martyred prelate began remembering him in these words:

> It helps, now and then, to step back and take a long
>   view.
> The kingdom is not only beyond our efforts,
> it is even beyond our vision.
>
> We accomplish in our lifetime only a tiny fraction
> of the magnificent enterprise that is God's work.
> Nothing we do is complete, which is a way of saying
> that the kingdom always lies beyond us.
> No statement says all that could be said.
> No prayer fully expresses our faith.
> No confession brings perfection.
> No pastoral visit brings wholeness.
> No program accomplishes the church's mission.
> No set of goals and objectives includes everything.
>
> This is what we are about.
> We plant the seeds that one day will grow.
> We water seeds already planted,
> knowing that they hold future promise.
>
> We lay foundations that will need further
>   development.
> We provide yeast that produces far beyond our
>   capabilities.

*We cannot do everything, and there is a sense of
    liberation
in realizing that. This enables us to do something,
and to do it very well. It may be incomplete,
but it is a beginning, a step along the way,
an opportunity for the Lord's grace to enter and do
    the rest.*

*We may never see the end results, but that is the
    difference
between the master builder and the worker.*

*We are workers, not master builders; ministers,
    not messiahs.
We are prophets of a future not our own.*

These wise words originated in a draft homily prepared
by the late Bishop Kenneth Untener, of Saginaw, Michigan,
when he was rector of the now defunct St. John Provincial
Seminary, for use by the Cardinal Archbishop of Detroit,
John Dearden, at a mass for deceased Detroit priests on
October 25, 1979, five months before Romero's death. They
spell out in the vocabulary of everyday disappointment and
frustration the implications of the Paschal Mystery for all
who believe that Jesus suffered, died, and rose again to make
a difference in their lives both here and hereafter.

A book edited by Robert Pelton, CSC, and titled,
*Archbishop Romero: Martyr and Prophet for the New
Millennium* is a collection of papers delivered at the
University of Notre Dame in the spring of 2005, marking the
twenty-fifth anniversary of Archbishop Romero's death. The
chapter, "Romero the Preacher," by Barbara E. Reid, OP,

documents the path—from Untener to Dearden, to admirers of Romero—that this remarkable prayer has taken.

It will, I believe, continue to make the rounds in the hearts of believers trying to make sense of the ups and downs in their own lives in a world where hatred seems unwilling to yield to love, and violence, for some diabolical reason, just won't let go.

33. Why the War on Terrorism Is Likely to Be a Long One

If you're wondering if the war on terrorism is likely to be a long one, take a look at Caryle Murphy's book, *Passion for Islam—Shaping the Modern Middle East.*

Murphy, a 1991 Pulitzer Prize winner for her reporting during Desert Storm, spent five years in Cairo, as bureau chief for the *Washington Post. Passion for Islam*—the title is drawn from a post-sentencing statement made in 1995 by a moderate Egyptian Islamist found guilty of "practicing democracy"—provides a useful interpretative framework for puzzled observers like myself who need help in understanding the Muslim world. The "passion" for Islam that Murphy observed up close in several Muslim countries is driving an attempt "to fuse two powerful desires, one for democratic government and the other for Islam to be their society's main reference point." This drive is being felt throughout an anything-but-unified Muslim world.

Ever since the exiled Ayatollah Ruhollah Khomeini returned home to lead Iran's Islamic revolution in 1979, Americans have been at a loss to understand clergy-turned-politicians claiming to rule in the name of God while encouraging mobs of Muslims in their fist-shaking threats to the "Great Satan." That started Caryle Murphy thinking about the need to gain a better understanding of the Islamic revival that all of us realize is happening and too few of us can even begin to figure out.

Her book provides a four-layer model for examination of the Islamic revival. It is presented in the context of three historical forces. The first is the evident reawakening and subsequent turmoil within Islam. The second historical force is the enduring presence of authoritarian Arab governments. The third is the shared failure to resolve the Israeli-Palestinian conflict. These forces, says Murphy, "have combined to create a combustible environment in the Middle East."

She then points to "four separate but overlapping levels" of Islam's ongoing revival since the 1970s. First she identifies "Pious Islam," an upsurge or "grassroots groundswell" of "women donning headscarves, more men shunning alcohol, and everyone more observant of religious rituals." Next comes "Political Islam," wherein "Islamist activists are seeking to wrest power from secular-oriented governments in order to implement a religious-based vision of an Islamic state and society." Third is "Cultural Islam," a resistance movement against Western cultural values. The fourth layer of Islamic renewal is theological—a "Thinking Islam" that is moving toward more enlightened and scientific interpretation of the Qur'an.

There is no Vatican for Islam and hence no possibility of an Islamist "Vatican Council" to produce a workable doctrine of religious freedom. Nor is there an Islamist John Courtney Murray to work out a theology of separation of mosque and state.

Muslims, as Caryle Murphy explains, "are in the throes of a historical resurgence of their faith." Islam, which is certainly not a single reality, "has become a template for the culturally confused, a language of protest for the politically frustrated, and a vision for nations adrift in a competitive world."

This author doesn't claim to understand the mind of Osama bin Laden, but she does understand the historical forces that helped shape today's Muslim radicals who are willing to kill and be killed in the name of Islam.

This rewarding read leaves no doubt that what we are calling a war on terrorism is going to last a long, long time.

34. Reading and Talking about Justice

A decade or so ago, thousands of people in Chicago began reading the same book at the same time. Harper Lee's 1960 novel *To Kill a Mockingbird* was Chicago Public Library Commissioner Mary Dempsey's choice for a seven-week project that brought readers together in homes, libraries, bookstores, and coffee shops to discuss the "doing-the-right-thing" themes in *Mockingbird*, a novel whose sales have topped thirty million over four decades. The novel deals with fairness, civil rights, and social justice. It is also, a psychiatrist who works with children told me when the book first appeared, "the best nontechnical exposition of the workings of the six-year-old mind" that he had ever seen.

Readers all remember the little girl, Scout, coming home after her first day in the first grade and announcing to her lawyer-father, Atticus, that she was not returning to school—ever. Why? Because the teacher told her she had to unlearn the way her father had taught her to read:

> [R]eading was just something that came to me....I could not remember when the lines above Atticus's finger separated into words, but I had stared at them all the evenings in my memory, listening...to anything Atticus happened to be reading when I crawled into his lap every night.

In an effort to get her to reconsider her decision not to return to school, Atticus reasoned with his daughter this way: "If you can learn a simple trick, Scout, you'll get along a lot better with all kinds of folks. You never really understand a person until you consider things from his point of view...until you climb into his skin and walk around in it."

As the story unfolds, Scout does indeed learn to "climb inside the skin" of others, especially two "mockingbird" characters, each innocent, harmless, and vulnerable, who are done in by an unjust and brutal society.

The first half of this novel portrays a nostalgic growing-up experience in a small Alabama town. The second half disposes of small-town Southern gentility to expose the harsh reality of prejudice and ignorance in ordinary folk. If the first part of the book can be called the education of a little girl, the last half of it could be labeled racism runs deep. It did then, in the story setting of the 1930s; it does now in cities all across the country.

For their citywide reading experience, Seattle, Buffalo, and Rochester read *A Lesson Before Dying*, by Ernest J. Gaines, another book about racial justice. Not a bad idea to get a few conversations going about racism in our cities. The right books can help.

"The one place where a man ought to get a square deal," says Atticus to his son Jem in *To Kill a Mockingbird*, "is in a courtroom, be he any color of the rainbow. But people have a way of carrying their resentments right into a jury box."

Good fiction holds up the mirror so we can take a peek and see ourselves as we really are. Good fiction also offers nourishing food for thought like this morsel that Atticus passed along to Scout: "[B]efore I can live with other folks I've got to live with myself. The one thing that doesn't abide by majority rule is a person's conscience."

There are lots of books with ideas worth talking about. There are a lot of cities where the talk needs to get started. Thanks, Seattle, Buffalo, Rochester, and Chicago for showing us the way.

35. Poetry Can Put a Needed Perspective on Memorial Day

Being named "Commonwealth Poet" by the Governor of Pennsylvania is not an empty honor. Sam Hazo learned that soon after being named state poet by Governor Robert P. Casey, who wasted no time in putting him to work. This distinguished Pittsburgh poet, a former Marine captain, was asked by the governor to write a poem that would honor all those Pennsylvanians who had received the Congressional Medal of Honor.

Dr. Hazo discovered that the Medal of Honor is our nation's highest award for valor in action against an enemy force. Selflessness and a concern for the safety of others were, he learned, constitutive elements of the valor this medal recognizes. So he went to work and crafted an opening line with which no one who has been in combat will disagree: "No soldiers choose to die." It (death), this poem continues, "is what they risk/ by being who and where they are."

Memorial Day calls attention to all those known and unknown "who's"—the honored and overlooked—who were in all those "wheres" that name the locations of this nation's battles. The latest entry to this national catalogue of courage is, of course, Iraq.

"It's what they dare/while saving someone else/whose life means suddenly as much to them as theirs/ or more," this poem goes on to say. Pure and simple, that's what valor is. Impressed with the purity of such valor, this ex-Marine's poetic pen raises a question about the "glory" of war: "To honor them, why speak of duty/or the will of governments?/ Think first of love each time you tell their story./It gives their sacrifice a name,/and takes from war its glory."

Memorial Day is a time to think of love. Love can be viewed as a deterrent to war. It can prompt open and reasonable minds to entertain the thought that war is now obsolete, no longer useful or justifiable as an instrument of change. Power, of course, is the ability to bring about or prevent change. If given a chance, love can bring about the change that war so clumsily, destructively, and unsuccessfully tries to achieve.

The harsh reality of heroic sacrifice "takes from war its glory." The sacrifice of heroes is a form of love that tells the fuller story that Memorial Day invites the American mind to ponder.

Jerry Colbert is executive producer of the National Memorial Day Concert, seen on PBS on the Sunday evening before Memorial Day. It is broadcast live each year from the West Lawn of the U.S. Capitol.

Several hundred thousand remembering and celebrating citizens spread blankets and picnic suppers on the Capitol lawn to enjoy the concert. Millions more across the country and around the world see it all on television.

Jerry Colbert looks upon his work as a ministry. Upon graduation many years ago from the College of the Holy Cross in Worcester, Massachusetts, Colbert served as a lay volunteer with the Jesuits in Baghdad, Iraq. Iraq is very much on his mind in recent years as he helps a nation remember its war dead and celebrate its freedom in the familiar setting of Washington's great monuments and memorials. The ministry dimension of this work, Colbert discovered, goes beyond helping a nation to remember past sacrifice and appreciate present freedom. He helps survivors grow through their grief and, along with others, dedicate themselves to the pursuit of peace and justice.

36. Peacemaking and the Beatitudes

A Catholic Peace Fellowship group that draws its membership from three suburban Washington, DC, parishes, invited me to give a lecture on Catholic social teaching several years ago. The topic: "The Beatitudes and Catholic Social Thought," a theme I had discussed in other lectures in earlier years. But the setting this time—an audience of Catholics committed to the promotion of peace in our day—was different.

The tone for the evening was set by a prayer service with appropriate Scripture passages, litanies, and prayers of petition that could have made some with military connections uncomfortable. In the audience was the daughter of Jack Seese, a friend of mine from high school days. He graduated in the Class of 1944 and was whisked away into army training for combat in Germany where, before his nineteenth birthday, he was wounded in action.

I followed the same path one year later—turned eighteen in May, graduated in June, and was in the army in July. I trained for jungle warfare in the Pacific with a view to the invasion of Japan. President Truman's decision to drop the atomic bomb on Hiroshima and Nagasaki altered that equation. It ended the war and sent me off to Germany for service throughout 1946 in the army of occupation.

So there I was sixty years later in St. Raphael's Parish Hall in Rockville, Maryland, to talk about the concise summary of what it means to be a Christian known as the Beatitudes. Prominent among them is a blessing on the "peacemakers." There are eight beatitudes in the Gospel of Matthew: the poor in spirit, those who mourn, the meek, those who hunger and thirst for justice, the merciful, the singlehearted, the peacemakers, and the persecuted.

A somewhat different version appears in the Gospel of Luke, a bit shorter and even more countercultural than Matthew's list. In Luke, the words speak simply and starkly of the poor, the hungry, the weeping, the hated, the excluded and insulted. Luke says poor, not poor in spirit, and he omits direct reference to peacemaking. He does, however, have Jesus say, "Love your enemies, do good to those who hate you, bless those who curse you, pray for those who mistreat you."

During the 2004 presidential election campaign in the United States, there was a lot of discussion about how Catholics should vote and how presidential candidates and other office seekers matched up against Catholic values. My suggestion was then (as it was again in 2008) to hold up the candidates and their party platforms against the background of the Beatitudes. There is no perfect match, of course, but this doesn't mean that the exercise is futile. It serves to remind that the core message of Christianity is summarized in the Beatitudes. It also encourages a second look (or see it again for the first time look) at the principles of Catholic social teaching, a body of doctrine that relates to issues raised in the Beatitudes.

Catholic social teaching offers *credenda* (propositions to be believed) and *agenda* (ideas to be acted upon). It touches upon: the dignity of the human person; respect for human life; the right of association; the right of participation; preferential love for the poor; solidarity; stewardship; subsidiarity; justice; and the common good.

My Rockville audience asked why peacemaking is not explicitly included in a body of doctrine that provides a place for just war theory. Good question. They also asked for an exact alignment between the eight Beatitudes and the principles of Catholic social teaching. Good project for religious educators in any place at any time.

PART FIVE
Church

37. Out-of-the-Box Thinking for Church Leadership

If you ever wonder why we don't have a Catholic C-SPAN (the cable satellite public affairs network), or a Catholic equivalent of the Mormon Tabernacle Choir, you are doing the kind of thinking that the U.S. Conference of Catholic Bishops never gets around to at its annual November meeting in Washington, DC. This is not necessarily because the bishops and their conference staff have "better things to think about." It's simply because they've got so many front-line, high priority things to discuss that they don't have time on their agenda for smaller, quieter ideas that could, if translated into programs, contribute to the vitality of the Church the conference exists to serve.

A great form of lay participation in the life of the Church would be out-of-the-box thinking that could lead the bishops to set up a task force or two during their annual meeting in Year One, and commission them to produce a report that could result in an action item on the November agenda two or three years later. Any action item would, of course, have to have budgetary legs to bring it to the floor for serious debate.

Out-of-the-box thinking would mean out-of-the-chancery, out-of-the-sanctuary, out-of-the-social-theological-liturgical-educational-and-public policy arenas where the bishops' agenda normally and quite properly sinks its roots. Those who come up with interesting small ideas (there are plenty of experts in the conference to generate the big ideas!) might be invited to take a place on a task force with the opportunity to speak up in support of their proposals in one of the November meetings.

What if there were a Catholic C-SPAN? C-SPAN is financed by the cable industry; it began in 1979 with four employees and one telephone line. What if there were on cable television a Catholic *Booknotes* every weekend? What if a Catholic C-SPAN had bureaus in Washington, New York, Boston, Chicago, New Orleans, Denver, San Francisco, and other Catholic centers of influence in between—South Bend, for example? Wouldn't it be great to be able to tune in to the classrooms, cultural centers, panel discussions, lectures, debates, and exhibitions in Catholic institutional settings? Catholic hospitals would surely have interesting fare to offer interested viewers. Just as C-SPAN is on Capitol Hill every day, a Catholic counterpart could cover the daily activities of the U.S. Conference of Catholic Bishops in Washington, and maybe even provide a regular call-in program with conservative, moderate, and progressive lines!

Those who admire the resourcefulness of the Church of Jesus Christ of Latter-Day Saints in bringing to the nation the beautiful voices of the Mormon Tabernacle Choir (while deriving a well-deserved public relations benefit in return), might sometimes ask: Why not a "National Catholic Chorale" with a home at the Basilica of the National Shrine of the Immaculate Conception in Washington, DC? The Church could surely use the public relations bonus and the nation would be enriched by the cultural contributions of Catholic singers and instrumentalists.

Just as there are many other places and events that could attract Catholic cable television cameras, there are also a lot of other small ideas worthy of consideration by the body of bishops for the betterment of both church and nation. The task force mechanism can be utilized at any time to put wheels under good ideas. Lots of good ideas are out there between the ears of thinking Catholics whose eyes would welcome a C-SPAN-like window on their Catholic world.

38. Listen to the Names We Call Ourselves

The names we call ourselves provide perspective on how we act within any system. There's talk these days about systemic change in the Church. I wonder if anyone is thinking about change in the names we call ourselves.

I've been called "Father" for almost fifty years in the system of ordained priestly service to the Catholic community. A child, speaking of me, once asked her mother, "Whose father is he?" The mother, a young widow I had helped when her husband died in an automobile accident, found herself saying, "Anybody who needs one."

Some lay Catholics and not a few non-Catholics are uncomfortable with the title "Father." I'd trade it for "Pastor" in the united church we all pray for, where Catholic priests, Lutheran pastors, and female ministers would not be separated by awkward nomenclature. Regrettably, we are not even close to having to face that issue now. All "Monsignors" can relax!

There is an apocryphal story told about a now deceased cardinal who thought of himself as a "prince of the Church." Speaking to his assembled priests, he mentioned something that happened in his morning prayer. "I asked our blessed Lord this morning what should I do about this," said the cardinal, "and Our Blessed Lord replied to me, 'Your Eminence'...." There is something of a flattening out, a delayering, taking place in the Church today. Don't mistake it for an erosion of authority. It is an emergence of humanity, human leadership, what some call "servant leadership." It's a movement of the Holy Spirit bringing leadership and followership closer together in a community called Church. It is giving the gate to both hypocrisy and hyperbole in clerical circles.

"I am Joseph, your brother," said the late Cardinal Joseph Bernardin when he first met his assembled priests in their cathedral in Chicago. Not Joe, but Joseph. Many priests and some laypersons addressed him that way during his years of service to the Church of Chicago.

Visitors to the cemetery at St. John's, the Benedictine Monastery in Collegeville, Minnesota, walk up a path and see on the hill above, stump-like granite crosses over the graves of the monks. Carved onto the back of the crossbar is the first name only. "Michael," "Godfrey," "Robert"— strong, stark, dignified, solemn. I would not be surprised to see a gradual shift in future years from an emphasis on formal ecclesiastical titles to simple and straightforward baptismal names in letters and conversation between the faithful and those ordained to serve them from positions of authority.

There is a deeply felt need among lay Catholics to be seen and heard by those in authority in the Church. There is poignancy often in their plea for improved communication. Some few are strident and demanding, but most, if I am not misinterpreting the voices I'm hearing, are loyal and loving in their insistence on being heard. It is something like the "mounting urgency" that the stage directions expect of Emily in Thornton Wilder's *Our Town* when, toward the end of the play, she says, "O Mama, just look at me one minute as though you really saw me....Mama, just for a moment...*Let's look at one another.*"

That's what Catholics are saying to their bishops today.

In a united church, there will be, I'm sure, a "Holy Father," who will be addressed as "Your Holiness." He will, I suspect, regard himself as occupying the center of a circle, not the top of a pyramid. The Church will be seen as a circle of service, clearly recognizable as the body of Christ, where all members will be seen, heard, and in the habit of listening to one another.

39. A Damaged Church in Need of Repair

Sin, sickness, and crime were all part of the clergy sex-abuse scandals that shocked the Catholic world in 2002. So are secrecy, arrogance, hypocrisy, and the violation of trust. Innocent victims suffered spiritual and psychological damage. We now have a damaged Church in need of repair, even though much of the damage was done decades ago.

Restitution, in the sense of making injured persons "whole" again, is an obligation to be met by responsible

Church officials who are wise enough to reject false accusations and humble enough to admit past mistakes. Reparation, in the sense of doing penance for sin, is a duty to be met by all of us. With regard to both restitution and reparation, it must be said that although only some are guilty, all are responsible. We are all in this together.

Sin calls for contrition, penance, and a firm purpose of amendment. Sickness, in the form of pedophilia and other sexual disorders, requires treatment. Crime calls for detection, conviction, and just punishment.

We must always be willing to forgive the sinner, compassionate enough to treat the ill, but wise enough to know that the sexual disorder known as pedophilia is an illness that bars the pedophile forever from all unsupervised contact with children. They cannot be cured of that disorder; they must, however, do everything possible to control it. Clear criminal behavior has to be reported to civic authorities as soon as it becomes known. Prison in some cases and public disgrace are part of the price that has to be paid.

A concerned but confused Catholic mother asked me when all this hit the headlines whether there is a connection between pedophilia and homosexuality. There is none. There are hetero- and homosexual, married and unmarried pedophiles; their victims are prepubescent males and females. Most of the cases of clergy sexual misconduct relate to inappropriate sexual contact with adults, male or female, although many notorious cases involve predatory homosexual activity with postpubescent boys and young men. Every case is shameful and regrettable, and patently unjust.

The Church is most alive in its parishes. The parishes live on the trust they place in their priests. Violations of that trust put the Church in critical condition at the turn of this present century and we are not yet out of what can only be called critical condition. The thousands of good and completely trustworthy priests now at work in parishes can bring us out of this crisis. The Church chooses her priests from men called to celibacy. Celibacy is not the cause of the crisis. Recommitment to celibacy will be part of the solution. This is not to say that in a world where "for God, all things are possible" (Matt 19:26), alternatives to an all-celibate, all-male priesthood will never be a fact of Catholic life. But we have to deal with a crisis right now and this raises the question of prayer and fasting for all of us, and much more careful screening of the men applying to seminaries and presenting themselves for ordination. Their sexual histories must be known; their commitment to celibacy must be unequivocal.

Respected Catholics began calling other Catholics in 2002 to withhold financial contributions to diocesan collections. This is unwise. Refusing to contribute means not having your protest known. Designate your gift through the diocese to a nearby Carmelite or Trappist monastery from where prayer and fasting energize the whole Church. Or designate the contribution for the poor as a means of registering your protest against secrecy or perceived mismanagement on the part of diocesan authorities. Yes, you will have to trust that your designation will be honored, but you will not have withheld support from a wounded community when it needs your prayer, fasting, and financial assistance.

Volumes could be written about this tragic episode in the life of the American Church. I'll stop here. But the crisis triggered new movements in the life of the Church. I'll discuss several of them in subsequent pages.

40. A Few "What-Ifs" for a Healthier, Safer Church

With the February 27, 2002, release by the U.S. Conference of Catholic Bishops of the John Jay study of clergy sex abuse along with the report of the National Review Board for the Protection of Children and Young People, American Catholics were encouraged to reflect on the causes of sexual abuse of minors by clergy. Many were stunned not just by the disclosure of abuse but at the extent of the mismanagement of this problem by Church officials over the years.

The report generated a series of expressed and unexpressed "what-ifs" in the minds of parishioners. This triggered thinking about structural adjustments to prevent a repetition of past mistakes and reduce the probability of any child ever again being victimized by any priest. Here are samples of some of that thinking.

What if every parish council, like every hospital board of directors, had a credentialing and quality assurance committee? Its job would be, among other things, to review the credentials and personnel files of any priest about to be assigned to a parish. He would be reviewed and rated by this committee before being accepted for ministry. For this screen to work, the confidential personnel file would have to be up to date. The diocesan bishop or provincial superior would have to cooperate and abide by the credentialing committee's decision.

If that "what-if" were a functioning reality in any diocese, the probability of a priest-predator being shuttled from parish to parish would be zero.

What if a bishop or admitting provincial felt obliged to know the sexual history of every candidate for admission to a seminary? This is admittedly intrusive and invasive of the privacy our culture prizes. No candidate would be forced, however, to continue, or even to begin to participate in this conversation, but the conversation should take place. Psychosexual health, like physical health, should be considered essential for admission to a seminary.

What if every bishop had an annual one-on-one accountability conversation with every priest in his diocese? It is obvious from revelations associated with the sex-abuse scandals that many bishops simply did not know their men. They did not know their strengths and weaknesses, their fears and hopes.

It is also obvious that some of the priest-perpetrators were not open to their bishops; they dissembled, hid, lied, and knowingly violated sacred trusts. Were bishops "too busy" with administrative matters to attend to the men under their jurisdiction? If so, would a scheduled, annual or semiannual, one-on-one conversation of accountability between priest and bishop close these gaps and provide a measure of safety for potential victims in the future? Without mutual trust, this won't work.

What if every diocese in the process of awaiting the appointment of a new bishop received public notification similar to the traditional publication of "banns" of marriage? Names of those under consideration for appointment as bishop (usually three) would be announced from every pulpit in the diocese from which they entered the seminary, the diocese where they currently serve, and the diocese to which they are being proposed for service as bishop. If this disclosure practice were in place, a man with a sexual misconduct skeleton in his closet would have to be uncommonly ambitious to run the risk of public embarrassment to himself and the Church.

What if diocesan and presbyteral councils really worked? What if the clergy accepted the fact that the parish is a "family-owned business" and all family members have a right to be kept informed on how the business is doing?

Enlightened criticism like that which emerged in the wake of the release of the John Jay report can bring about structural adjustments, which eventually will mean safer children in a healthier Church.

41. Voice of the Faithful
as a Social Movement

There are three broad ways to think about social change—fatalism, reform, or revolution. The first is a do-nothing, wait-and-see approach. The second presupposes the possibility, and then focuses on the reality of new ways of doing things as well as on steps that will lead to significant change. The third is simply an overthrow or demolition approach to the problem.

The often praised, often criticized lay movement in the Church known as Voice of the Faithful (VOTF) is a reform movement. A book by William D'Antonio and Anthony Pogorelc, *Voices of the Faithful: Loyal Catholics Striving for Change*, is not only a sociological study of the origins of VOTF, viewed as an incipient social movement in the Church in response to the clerical sex-abuse scandal that became public in 2002, but it also offers, through reflective chapters written by six scholar-commentators, an analytical critique of the early stages of this movement.

As one of the many active VOTF members interviewed by the authors said, "I think many of the local chapters have had a hard time figuring out their function. Once they get together, express discontent, make ties with the survivors groups, and try to help, what else do you do? This is their question, and they haven't had good guidance on that."

There is a well-known American penchant to substitute blame for analysis. Blame is employed sparingly in this sociological study. Analysis is offered in a way that will be valuable to VOTF chapters around the country as well as to wary bishops and priests who tend to go on the defensive whenever a VOTF banner is raised.

The demographic data presented by D'Antonio and Pogorelc are instructive—the movement is 60 percent female; it lacks youth and Hispanic participation, and is well above the national Catholic average in mass attendance and educational attainment. These facts can be ignored by friends of the movement only at the risk of jeopardizing its future. Enemies of the movement would do well to heed the data if they are serious about meeting the pastoral needs of all Catholics.

This study finds that faithful Catholic people want to have a voice in the selection of their parish priests and local bishops; they want a voice in deciding how parish and diocesan income is spent.

In a 1970 book by economist Alfred Hirschman titled *Exit, Voice, and Loyalty*, the threat of exit over against the pull of loyalty to an organization is examined in selected business firms, voluntary associations, and political organizations. Notice the fulcrum position of "voice" in that triad of "exit, voice, and loyalty," and then apply that triad to the case of the Catholic Church after the abuse scandals.

"Hirschman is looking at the interplay between two options that members have when an organization to which they belong is experiencing difficulty," writes William Gamson, a contributor to the D'Antonio-Pogorelc study. "They can leave and put their energy into some other organization or into other pursuits; or they can try to change the organization—that is what Hirschman means by exercising voice."

That is why voice—well-informed, incisive, articulate, respectful and, it must be said, appropriately modulated—is so critically important to whatever VOTF proposes to do in the years ahead.

It is worth noting that structural change never happens suddenly, but structural adjustments are happening all the time. Enlightened criticism from VOTF will bring about structural adjustments, which eventually will lead to noticeable change. For this to happen, however, the movement needs staying power and its critics need patience. Neither can afford to ignore or attack the other.

42. Executive Courage to the Rescue

"Stop Stonewalling on Reform," reads the scolding June 17, 2002, editorial. "Each day brings news of yet another... scandal."

"A Ripe Time for Reform," was the headline over an editorial in an earlier issue of the same magazine. It opened with these words, "The ground is shifting beneath the foundations of..."

You may think you can complete that sentence, but you could be wrong. This is *Business Week*, not *America* or *Commonweal* that I'm citing. American business, not the Catholic Church in America, is the object of this editorial criticism.

Consider the front cover of *Business Week* on May 6, 2002: "The Crisis in Corporate Governance: Excessive Pay. Weak Leadership. Corrupt Analysts. Complacent Boards. Questionable Accounting. How to Fix the System." One week later the same magazine had this on its cover: "Wall Street: How Corrupt Is It?" Another *Business Week* cover story pointed to "betrayed" investors who have been "misled by Wall Street, corporations, accountants, and the government. The strength of the recovery hinges on winning back their confidence." Finally, the *Business Week* cover on June 24, 2002, highlighted a "Special Report" on "Restoring Trust in Corporate America: Why CEOs Must Speak Up; How Institutional Investors Are Pushing Reform."

The Church can learn a lot from what analysts say about corporate corruption. Religious commentators call the clergy sex-abuse scandal the most serious crisis the Catholic Church in America has ever faced. *Business Week*'s May 6 report says, "Faith in Corporate America hasn't been so strained since the early 1900s, when the public's furor over the monopoly powers of big business led to years of trust-busting by Theodore Roosevelt." The parallels are striking.

Substitute bishop for CEO and diocese for corporation as you read these accounts of the present predicament in which the American business system finds itself. There is "widespread suspicion and distrust" in both arenas, where decision makers have committed "egregious breaches of trust by cooking the books and shading the truth"—words taken from the business press, but applicable on the ecclesiastical side of the street.

No small embarrassment for the Church to find itself compared with Enron and Arthur Andersen. Ironically, the Andersen CEO used religious language to explain his resignation as a "sacrifice" for the good of his employees.

Writer Thomas Keneally acknowledges that he separated himself from the ranks of practicing Catholics years ago when he became convinced that "behind the compelling mystery of Catholicism...lay a cold and largely self-interested corporate institution."

The executives of that "corporate institution," the bishops, not yet ready to perform surgery on themselves at their 2002 meeting in Dallas, are back in their chanceries seriously trying to repair the damage and prevent further harm. Some are "pushing reform." Most, having heard the victims tell their stories, are closer to their people and realize that "recovery hinges on winning back their confidence."

Although the bishops know that their "corporate institution" has a soul and lives on God's promise to be with the Church until the end of time, they have to begin thinking systemically. They should note what the business system is doing in its effort to recapture lost trust. Transparency, accountability, reform of governance, servant leadership, and patient listening are coming to the rescue of the business system. All of these, along with humility, penance, and prayer provide a formula to be followed by all who love the Church enough to change it. Our Church will become stronger in its broken places if executive courage, not privilege, becomes the order of everyday ecclesiastical life.

43. Villanova and Church Management

From his observation post in Wilmington, North Carolina, Paul Wilkes moves around the country to study the quality of congregational life in various faith communities. Prominent among his eighteen nonfiction books is *Excellent Catholic Parishes: The Guide to Best Places and Practices.* He also wrote *And They Shall Be My People: An American Rabbi and His Congregation* and has created a parish revitalization curriculum called "New Beginnings 101, 201, 301: A New Way of Living a Christian Life."

So it was no surprise to see Paul Wilkes on the Villanova University campus in March 2005 to deliver a public lecture that helped launch Villanova's new Center for the Study of Church Management (CSCM). Wilkes took an unusual approach to the topic of stewardship. He showed how a renewed understanding of stewardship as a personal, individual, lay responsibility can create a vibrant, communal, parochial reality. You don't have to wait for pastor, parish council, or general consensus to get up and running; just take your own good idea, bring it to the attention of fellow parishioners, and welcome the good things that will inevitably happen.

"If you build it—whatever that parish-based 'it' may be—they will come," said Wilkes. Anyone can do it. Ignore the nay-sayers; just go ahead and start your own community-building ball rolling. Next thing you know parish revitalization is underway.

He could not have known the parallel to the origins of the Center that was sponsoring his lecture. As those familiar with university life know, any creative faculty member with a good idea, a file cabinet, and a letterhead can start up a Center for the Study of…just about anything. Start-up financial support from foundations or friends, or even from the university itself, moves the project down the runway and facilitates the take-off. But the pilot, navigator, baggage handler, and flight attendant are normally just one person—a generous visionary who is willing to "build it" so that others may come.

The visionary at Villanova is Dr. Charles Zech, a professor of economics, who saw the need for the Church in the United States to have a place to turn to when the management malfunctions of recent years made it painfully and patently clear that there is a need for research and education in the area of church management. Best practices for parishes, sound business procedures for dioceses, mapping of all the cultural, financial, and demographic variables that constitute the choppy waters through which the organizational Church is now attempting to find its way, all point to the need for an academic center where blame is no substitute for analysis and answers are available for those who recognize their need for help.

Even though we joke that in economics, nothing is certain, anything is possible, and everything depends on everything else, it is indeed possible to apply tested academic methods to meet the challenges of church management. The task of sorting out problems through research and then laying out an education program for interested pastors, lay associates, and diocesan professionals is the mission of Villanova's CSCM.

The Center sponsored a workshop on civil and labor law for parishes one month prior to the Wilkes lecture. There was a summer management-training institute on campus the following summer for diocesan officials from around the country. It covered topics ranging from servant leadership, to planning, budgeting, financial accountability, communications, and a variety of human resource issues. The summer institute has been repeated in subsequent years. Villanova now has a fully accredited degree program—a master's degree in church management—offered through the University's business school. I know about all this because I serve on the Center's national advisory board and teach in the summer institute.

Other universities like Notre Dame, Boston College, and St. Thomas in the Twin Cities are into management education for Church employees. The need for this service is obvious in the wake of mismanagement associated with the sex-abuse scandals. Financial fraud in dioceses and Church organizations is the next great scandal that will sound a wake-up call to those who are responsible for the quality of management in church-operated organizations.

44. Needed: Better Organization of National Collections

The Catholic Church in the United States represents the largest unorganized philanthropic potential in the world. That problem is both sad and fixable. We, as a national Church community, don't raise money efficiently and effectively. We can fix that problem by a simple organizational adjustment. Think of it as "Second Collection, Second Sunday."

I believe it would triple or quadruple the dollar totals our twelve national collections now produce.

On twelve days spread across the year, church-going Catholics have a so-called second collection opportunity to contribute to good causes. Each is presented as an "appeal" approved by the U.S. Conference of Catholic Bishops. Content and scheduling of the presentations are somewhat hit and miss. The "case" for giving is often vague and unpersuasive, and sometimes insufficiently audible or visible to work its way into the worshiper's awareness.

These twelve national collections are

1. Aid to the Church in Central and Eastern Europe;
2. Black and Indian Missions;
3. Catholic Campaign for Human Development;
4. Catholic Communication Campaign;
5. Catholic Home Missions Appeal;
6. Catholic Relief Services;
7. Catholic University of America;
8. Church in Latin America;
9. Holy Land;
10. Peter's Pence (Collection for the Holy Father);
11. Retirement Fund for Religious;
12. World Mission Sunday.

An online visit to www.usccb.org/nationalcollections/ncde scriptons.shtml will tell you more about each.

Ten of these collections are taken up on Sundays; two on weekdays—Ash Wednesday for the Church in Central and Eastern Europe, Good Friday for the Holy Land.

If the second Sunday of each month were designated for a special national collection, worshipers might begin to carry a bit more cash or bring a checkbook to church on those days. They might find their philanthropic thinking stretching beyond parochial boundaries at those times, not to the detriment of income to the parish, however, because it would indeed be a second collection. Literally and figuratively, the local parish would be first at the plate.

Some parishes have no second collections. Let them split or tithe their single collection with the special-purpose beneficiary on that Sunday. Some take up the second immediately after the first; not a great idea. Priests often say they don't like to talk about money. Bishops get opposition from their pastors when changes concerning collections are proposed and when directives go out for new or emergency collections.

"Second Collection, Second Sunday" could eliminate the need to "talk about money" much beyond a simple announcement. A week before, diocesan newspapers and parish bulletins could carry a well-reasoned and worded "case" for the special need, written by professionals associated with the beneficiary organization.

Where a diocese has television contact or radio outreach to Catholics, word about an upcoming collection can go out in the preceding week. Posters, PowerPoint presentations, flyers, envelopes, and any other explanatory material that would focus attention and highlight the need could be sent in advance to all the parishes by the beneficiary office or organization. Each beneficiary could promote its own special Sunday.

Here's a possible schedule: January, Latin America; February, Central and Eastern Europe; March, the Holy Land; April, Catholic Relief Services; May, Catholic Communication Campaign; June, the Holy Father; July, Catholic Home Mission; August, Black and Indian Missions; September,

Catholic University; October, World Missions; November, Campaign for Human Development; and December, the Retirement Fund for Religious.

The Administrative Board of the U.S. Conference of Catholic Bishops could rearrange this schedule. The point to be made is that a fixed schedule must be established if the needed funds are going to be raised. This would be a demonstration of good management and good stewardship on the part of Church leadership where, regrettably, the blame has to fall for the poor results that are so painfully evident to anyone who examines the record of Catholic fundraising on a national scale.

45. Have You Ever Been Asked to Evaluate a Homily?

It takes a bit of courage to invite homily evaluations from a parish congregation. But it is happening at a Catholic parish that will, for purposes of this essay, remain nameless simply to protect the innovative pastor from clerical colleagues who may not think this is such a great idea, and also to curb any tendency toward pride on the part of his cooperating parish council.

In the pews one Sunday a few years ago parishioners found the following form:

To All Who Worship Here...

Please take a moment to evaluate the homily you just heard and send your comments back to us at your convenience. This form is simple. The brief time it will take you to fill it out will amount to a big assist to your parish homilists. Many thanks!

Homily Evaluation Form

Here are my comments on the homily I heard on ❑ [date] at the ❑ [time] Mass.

1. I would rate the homily as excellent ❑; good ❑; fair ❑; poor ❑

2. I could hear the homily easily ❑; with difficulty ❑; hardly at all.

3. The homily ❑ was, or ❑ was not, well organized.

4. The topic of the homily was ❑, or was not ❑, appropriate.

5. The homily was too long ❑, too short ❑, just about right ❑ in length.

6. The central point made by the homilist was:

7. I would recommend that the homilist consider...

8. In future homilies, I would like to hear something said about...

Many thanks for your help!

The form indicates that any additional comments would be welcome and could be noted on the reverse side of the evaluation sheet. Respondents were told that there was no need to sign the form. They were asked to mail it back to the pastor or drop it in the collection basket. Moreover, the form is available on the parish Web site for use at any time. The printed version, parishioners were told, would be distributed by the director of liturgy periodically throughout the year with no prior notification given to the homilists.

Needless to say, the people were pleased to be asked and happy to participate. Not surprisingly, comments have been overwhelmingly constructive and for the most part positive; they have served, in the main, to encourage the homilists and lift the level of preaching in the parish.

This commendable practice is not something ordinarily taught in seminaries but it is routinely recommended in business schools. Any service-rendering agency welcomes client or customer feedback. Any company that puts a product on the market wants to know whether it is ringing up positive or negative marks on the customer-satisfaction register.

No need to hesitate to call a parish a service-rendering agency. Nor is it wise for any pastor to be unconcerned with product quality. To take another page from the business management literature, who should be surprised to find improvement on the parish's bottom line once the practice of homily evaluation is routine, regular, and a normal part of pastoral practice?

PART SIX
Public Policy

46. National Service Should Be as Visible as the Post Office

When *Time* published a late-summer cover story in 2007 calling for a dramatic expansion of national service, Republican presidential candidate Mitt Romney was asked what he thought of the idea. He replied that he was still considering his position on that issue. That response prompted me to recall that the candidate's father, former Michigan governor and one-time GOP presidential hopeful George Romney, was a strong supporter of voluntary service by Americans of all age groups.

"National service should be as visible as the Post Office," George Romney used to say. By that, he meant that a logo as recognizable as the one on mail boxes and postal workers' sleeves should be on the backs and letterheads of citizens from coast to coast who shared a commitment to helping out wherever help was needed. He favored educational incentives, but thought about service in a wider framework than just some kind of student-aid program for former volunteers who, after service, would go to college and get on with their lives. Citizens of all ages have a responsibility to serve, he said.

I served with the elder Romney on the board of the Commission on National and Community Service, which began in the administration of President George H. W. Bush, and morphed into the Corporation on National Service in the administration of President Bill Clinton.

The *Time* cover story was remarkably hopeful and helpful in putting the voluntary national service issue on the public policy agenda. It calls for the next president to initiate a ten-point plan for universal voluntary service.

Step one would be to create a "national service baby bond." With the birth of every American baby, the federal government would put five thousand dollars in that child's name in a trust fund. Interest would accrue and the account would be worth approximately nineteen thousand dollars when the child reached age twenty. Between the ages of eighteen and twenty-five, the money could be accessed on one condition—that the young man or woman would commit one year to community or military service. After service, the money could be used for education, to start a business, or to make a down payment on a home. No service, no benefit.

Time's plan would establish a cabinet-level Department of National Service under which existing service programs like AmeriCorps and the National Senior Volunteer Corps would be expanded. New programs would be introduced: an education corps, an institute of summer service for teenagers, a health corps, a green corps, and a new rapid-response reserve corps to do the kind of things that are typically done so poorly in the wake of national disasters like Hurricane Katrina.

Two additional ideas are offered: establish a United States Public Service Academy (like West Point or Annapolis), and create a Baby-Boomer Education Bond. An estimated seventy-eight million baby boomers will be eligible to retire over the next twenty years. The boomers could, under this plan, claim a scholarship (an educational savings account) of one thousand dollars for every five hundred hours of community service they complete. The dollars accrued could be used to educate the volunteers' children or grandchildren or any other student they so designate.

What about the cost? Not insignificant, but not unaffordable. Moreover, like the post-World War II G.I. Bill of Rights, there will be a return to the federal treasury in the form of income taxes on higher wages earned in function of the higher education beneficiaries receive, not to mention the savings to the nation in the form of service voluntarily rendered.

As they used to say in my old neighborhood, I'll vote for that!

47. Reflections on Politics and the Common Good

Catholics in Alliance for the Common Good is the carefully chosen title of a Washington-based organization that aims to link the tradition of Catholic social teaching to political debate in the United States. Care has been taken not to misrepresent this organization as officially and formally Catholic. It is just a modest movement involving ordinary Catholics who are familiar with the Church's social doctrine and intent on letting the light of that doctrine shine on the issues that too often divide us as a nation.

There is a baseline description of the common good sketched out in the Second Vatican Council's *Pastoral Constitution on the Church in the Modern World*, where the common good is described as "the sum total of social conditions which allow people, either as groups or as individuals, to reach fulfillment more fully and more easily" (no. 26).

Those "social conditions" have a way of emerging as topics for debate every four years in American presidential politics. For instance, the 2007 statement from the United States Conference of Catholic Bishops called "Forming Consciences for Faithful Citizenship: A Call to Political Responsibility" (www.faithfulcitizenship.org), states:

> As we all seek to advance the common good—by defending the inviolable sanctity of human life from the moment of conception until natural death, by defending marriage, by feeding the hungry and housing the homeless, by welcoming the immigrant and protecting the environment—it is important to recognize that not all possible courses of action are morally acceptable. We have a responsibility to discern carefully which public policies are morally sound. Catholics may choose different ways to respond to compelling social problems, but we cannot differ on our moral obligation to help build a more just and peaceful world through morally acceptable means, so that the weak and vulnerable are protected and human rights and dignity are defended. (no. 20)

In effect, the bishops are saying that there is need to connect the Church's social *credenda* (that which is to be believed) with the Church's social *agenda* (that which is to be done), and this agenda will coincide, often point for point, with the issues that find their way into political party platforms and partisan debates. Differences will, of course, surface on the recommended ways to move toward the desired ends.

A helpful step in framing the questions for debate, it seems to me, is to start thinking about a time-honored expression in Catholic social thought, namely, the "social question." What is the social question for our day?

At the most general level, I think the social question is: *How can the human community of persons, neighborhoods, and nations live together in peace secured by justice?* The protection of fundamental human dignity requires that the question be asked. The organization of human life requires that it be asked and applied in all areas of human activity.

Every significant social question can be traced to fault lines in human institutions. Only by working within those institutions can the fault lines be repaired. Only by participation in human processes, political for the most part, can we create new institutions that will provide just exchanges, promote just relationships, and foster peace. This is why Catholics in Alliance came into being. See for yourself at www.catholicsinalliance.org.

In the tradition of Catholic social thought, "solidarity" is a moral category that relates to the common good. An "alliance" for the common good is one way of encouraging solidarity and turning that powerful notion as a searchlight on social problems that await a political solution.

48. Social Credits for Stronger Families

There is no economic incentive for a natural parent to stay at home to care for his or her own child. Employ a babysitter, nanny, or a housekeeper in your home while you're at work, and you can deduct that payment as a business expense from your taxable income. If you stay at home to do the job yourself, you get no break.

No one I know is complaining about this, but some think it odd that there is no economic incentive for parents, who are normally best qualified to handle the childcare responsibility, to give it their full-time attention. No one disputes that children are "priceless" and society's future depends on the quality of care they receive. But neither is anyone providing financial help for parents who would rather be at home with their kids than in paid employment outside the house.

Social theorists have for years been offering possible solutions, but these proposals have not been heard. Perhaps the acoustics will improve. If that happens, an idea worth considering would be one that Neil Gilbert proposed in *Capitalism and the Welfare State* (1983). Let a full-time homemaker receive a federal "social credit" for each year spent at home with children who are under seventeen. Accumulated credits would either pay for higher education or entitle the stay-at-home parent to preferred hiring status in the federal civil service once the kids are raised and the parent is ready to return to work. Like the G.I. Bill, this benefit would compensate a citizen for time spent out of the workforce but in service to the nation. (How better to serve the nation than to devote full time to the preparation of its next generation?)

In Gilbert's scheme, each unit of social credit (one per child per year of full-time care) could be exchanged for either "(a) tuition for four units of undergraduate academic training, (b) tuition for three units of technical school training, (c) tuition for two units of graduate education, or (d) an award of one-fourth of a preference point on federal civil service examination." The parent is the implied beneficiary of the tuition grant in this scenario. The policy would surely be more attractive if an option to designate the homemaker's child as the educational beneficiary were made explicit. Then, instead of going to work "to put the kids through college," the second paycheck earner in a family could stay at home and achieve the same result.

The social credit doesn't discourage outside work. It simply provides an incentive to parents who might prefer homemaking to labor market activity. It doesn't confine women to the kitchen; men could choose to remain home and earn the same social credit. Not a perfect solution by any means for single moms, but some might find it helpful. Nor is it the answer for the working poor who, credits or not, could not afford not to work. But a single policy idea can hardly be expected to bear the full freight of all public policies needed to help poor families.

If this one option were available, it would be just that—an option, not an enforced condition. Any able-bodied male or female, rich or poor, could still choose to work full time, assuming full-time employment opportunities are available.

But the question remains: Is what we're doing now the best way to provide for our kids? I don't think the nation would give an unqualified affirmative reply. Creative social policy should be coming up with new answers. Elected representatives should be keeping their ears open for new ideas aimed at strengthening the family.

49. The Beatitudes and the Ballot Box

More and more Catholic conversations in any election season tend to center on religion and politics. That seems natural enough when campaigns and elections are in the news, but I'm wondering how Catholics would answer the question posed in a daily newspaper headline I saw not long ago: "Does God Belong in Politics?"

"Yes, of course," I found myself saying, "politics is people and God is in all people, so surely God belongs in politics." Without the people, how can God's will work in our world? If God is present in every person, how can God not be in politics?

We all pray each day, "Thy kingdom come," and know that it is a kingdom of love, justice, and peace that's been promised to us. We also know that the kingdom is the "reign of God," and that God reigns when our wills—individually and collectively—are in proper alignment with his. That's why reasoned, well-constructed, moral arguments are so important in the formation of public policy. Threat, force, and ridicule won't do it; moral reasoning will.

When Jesus stepped into his public life (Mark 1:14) he announced that the kingdom of God is "at hand"; he added, "repent, therefore, and believe the Gospel." I often think that it is tragic that a kingdom of love, justice, and peace has been "at hand" these many centuries but not yet grasped. I can only conclude that the delay in the coming of the promised kingdom is our refusal to "repent," to accept a value reversal, an attitudinal turnaround in response to Gospel values. This would convince us to lower the barriers within ourselves, namely, the opposites of love, justice, and peace that we harbor within, and thus open ourselves, individually and as a nation, to the promised kingdom that will indeed come, but only in God's own time and God's own way. Politics is part of the process that should be moving us in the right direction, but I'm not at all encouraged by the quality of reasoning that I find in most political debates.

Although there is a separation of church and state that is quite appropriate in this country, there is no separation between church and society. The Church, in my view, should be doing a better job in communicating Gospel values to society and then trusting society to make political decisions that are consistent with those values.

I think it is inaccurate to speak of "building" the king-dom. We can, as the popular hymn puts it, "build the City of God," but not the kingdom. All we can do is lower the barriers within ourselves to the coming of the promised kingdom; we cannot build what only God can give.

There is work to be done now in building the City of God and the political agenda is not unrelated to that work. Issues on the political agenda are multiple and diverse. No one issue alone will pave a sure and smooth road for the coming of the promised kingdom.

I know of one priest who, speaking from the side of reli-gion to the issues being debated in the 2004 and 2008 presi-dential campaigns, held up the Beatitudes (Matt 5:1–12) as a checklist. How does a given candidate or political party fare in that comparison? Few serious faith-committed voters, who are doing their best to assimilate Gospel values and bring them to life in this imperfect world, will say they've found a perfect fit.

The Church should stay out of partisan politics but not hesitate for a moment to suggest that Beatitude values belong in a good society, and that Beatitude principles can inform the moral reasoning needed to shape solid public policies. That's surely a good way for Catholics to help to build a better world.

50. Teacher Tax Credits

Education and taxes are hot-button political issues in almost all political campaigns. After the campaign, successful candidates then have to shift gears from politics to governance in order to deliver on their promises.

President George W. Bush had both at the top of his "to do list" when he moved into the Oval Office. He wanted to lower taxes and raise educational standards and performance. One policy initiative that can do both is something he never thought of, but I want to recommend it here.

It is the notion of a teacher tax credit. You can't improve education without attracting and retaining better teachers. Chances of holding better teacher talent in the schools would be enhanced by the teacher tax credit.

Not to be confused with tuition tax credits, teacher tax credits would apply only to teachers, say, those with two years of experience under supervision, who have demonstrated both their competence and their commitment to the classroom. Each would be entitled to take a credit, which is not a deduction from taxable income but a subtraction from the final tax bill, from the amount after deductions that the taxpayer is obliged to pay. This would be, in effect, a pay raise for teachers. The raise would not be at the expense of the already strained public purse in local and state jurisdictions that support the public schools. Neither would it come to private school teachers out of higher tuition payments from already burdened parents.

It would come, of course, from the federal government, but not as a spending item. It would be an investment. The solid, conservative principle at work here would be the same as the principle underlying investment tax credits that have been given to businesses over the years. Add a new plant or equipment, says the government to the entrepreneur, enlarge the productive capacity of the economy in your small way, and you will be entitled to an investment tax credit. The payback to government comes through increased productivity and future income-tax payments from the earnings of the business and of those whose jobs are associated with the new plant and new equipment.

Teachers open up minds. Teachers communicate knowledge, not just techniques. Well-educated minds generate new marketable ideas that expand economic activity. Who does more to enlarge the productive capacity of the nation than teachers? Why not an investment-like tax credit for them?

Is it fair to single out teachers for this tax break? I think it is. The profession is underpaid relative to its importance. Teachers serve the national interest in a special and privileged way. Why not put some money under the nation's thanks, why not enhance the prestige of the profession with higher pay?

Is this a scheme to favor private or parochial schools? No. Any certified teacher in any accredited classroom would qualify. Teachers only? What about administrators and staff?

Let the legislators decide. What about the amount? Let the writers of tax legislation with the help of the Congressional Budget Office decide. Try a four thousand- or five thousand-dollar credit for size and let the experts do the arithmetic.

If anyone says the cost to the federal Treasury is too high, then both the nation and its president will have to scale down their assessments of and rhetoric about the importance of the work teachers do and try to figure out some other way of finding and retaining competent people to do it.

Education is overdiscussed and undervalued in this country. As a nation, we are seriously underinvested in human capital. We improve human capital through education. Improved human capital leads to greater productivity. Greater productivity leads to higher incomes. Higher incomes provide an enlarged pool of taxable funds from which government can retrieve the revenue needed to finance better teaching in better schools. But that won't happen without better people more deeply committed to the task of teaching. Teacher tax credits can make that happen.

51. The Politics of Abortion

By a curious coincidence, on March 13, 2003, the very day the Senate passed, 64–33, a bill banning partial-birth abortions, I received in the mail from a friend in Pittsburgh a copy of a 1995 speech by then Pennsylvania Governor Robert P. Casey entitled, "Proudly Pro-Life in the Realm of Politics."

Newspaper reports on the Senate vote noted that two Senate Democrats, Kerry of Massachusetts and Edwards of North Carolina, who were then presidential contenders, were absent that day. The two other Senate Democratic presidential hopefuls, Lieberman of Connecticut and Graham of Florida, voted against the ban.

"Where, today, is conscience calling us?" asked Governor Casey in 1995. "What is the deepest source of unease?" he asked. "I believe the great majority of Americans know the answer."

He went on to say, "The silent figure at the center of our great cultural debate is the unborn child....It is, for me, the bitterest of ironies that abortion on demand found refuge in the national Democratic Party—my party, the party of the weak and powerless. To me, protecting the unborn child follows naturally from everything I know about my party and my country."

Sixteen Democrats joined forty-eight Republicans in voting for the ban on partial-birth abortion. The House passed the same bill. The president signed it into law. But abortion on demand, except for partial-birth abortion, continues to enjoy constitutional protection under Roe v. Wade.

"Abortion is an issue like few others we have ever faced," said Governor Casey in 1995. "Other causes demand commitment; abortion demands complicity. Other causes survive by virtue of energy and attention. The survival of the abortion industry depends upon avoidance and silence." (Source for Governor Casey quotes are from Address by Governor Robert P. Casey delivered at the University of Notre Dame; http.ethicscenter.nd.edu/archives/casey1995)

The irenic voice of John Carr, secretary of the U.S. Conference of Catholic Bishops' Office of Social Development and World Peace, spoke to both political parties in remarks made at a Washington meeting of Catholic social action workers when this issue was in the news. Catholics are having difficulty these days in finding a political home, he said. "There are very few organizations that actively fight abortion and actively fight capital punishment, that actively work for family leave and actively support family choice in education, that oppose the administration's stealth plans to undermine the [welfare] safety net, and for the same reasons support the Faith-Based Initiative.

"On the left," continued Carr, "our friends say, 'We love what you are doing on the death penalty, we love that you're one of the few voices standing up against this war, we love that you're trying to fix the [welfare reform] bill, but when you get to that abortion stuff, stop trying to impose your values on us.'"

Turning to criticism of Catholics from the political right, Carr said, "when you stand up for human life—even including those on death row—that's politics."

Then, as if he were reading from Governor Casey's text, Carr let the Democrats have it. "What do they stand for, except abortion on demand? In the last election, you couldn't figure it out. They seem to have lost their voice, if not their values."

If Robert P. Casey were still alive, he would direct our attention to the unborn child, "the silent figure at the center of our great cultural debate." He would say, as he said in that 1995 speech, "What is called for now is leadership— moral leadership of a high order. Leadership, with generosity and understanding, sending a message of civility and respect for opposing views, a message that bespeaks a true sense of community."

Let politicians who want to lead us sift through that message to find some principles, platform planks, and a place to stand.

Many Americans, including President Barack Obama, need a change of heart on this issue. His heart and the heart of the nation he was elected to lead in 2008 have to be open to "the silent figure at the center of our great cultural debate," namely, "the unborn child." Open hearts could lead to an opening of eyes, ears, and minds to a reasonable solution to a national problem that will continue to trouble us until we, as a nation, face up to the question Governor Casey raised in 1994, namely, "Where, today, is conscience calling us?"

52. Potatoes and Political Will

Every St. Patrick's Day I find myself wondering when Irish Americans will let the message from the potato on their dinner plates prompt them to take effective action to reduce world hunger.

Even though it was reported a few years ago that per-capita potato consumption in Ireland is declining, here in this country the potato—baked, boiled, mashed, but never fried—is a prominent part of the March 17 dinner gatherings of "Friendly Sons" (and those "daughters" able to break through the barriers) who honor St. Patrick and celebrate their Irish heritage in hotel ballrooms across the nation. Part of that heritage is the memory of bands of starving people who roamed the roads of Ireland in October 1846, "more like famishing wolves than men," according to one observer.

In 1849, Michael Shaughnessey, Assistant Barrister in County Mayo, passed from town to town on his circuit and everywhere saw children who were "almost naked, hair standing on end, eyes sunken, lips pallid, protruding bones of little joints visible." He asked himself, writes Cecil Woodham-Smith in *The Great Hunger*, "Am I in a civilized country and part of the British Empire?" He was, of course, on the "Emerald Isle," blackened by blighted potato fields in 1845 and 1846.

Curiously, it was a Daniel Shaughnessey (any relation?), who served as executive director of President Carter's Commission on World Hunger. That commission's report recommended that the United States "make the elimination of hunger the primary focus of its relationship with the developing world beginning with the decade of the 1980s." Millions of hungry people are still waiting for that to happen.

Hunger today is qualitatively different, of course, from potato famine hunger. Chronic undernourishment best describes the problem of world hunger in our time. Today's problem calls for political will as well as the application of available technical solutions. But where is the political will?

If Irish Americans in the U.S. Congress, and there are many there, do not take the lead in developing this nation's political will to do its fair share in combating hunger, who will? What other immigrant group left so many famished behind and brought so many fevered with them only to die on the way or soon after arrival as an ultimate consequence of the potato failure over there?

Potatoes on the plates of banqueting Irish Americans can recall, for anyone willing to remember, that hundreds of thousands, probably more than a million, Irish men and women died from starvation and disease related to the Great Hunger.

British lawmakers lined up at that time on the side of protectionism and laissez-faire. "You cannot answer the cry of want by a quotation from political economy," complained Sir Randolf Routh, chairman of the relief commission, to British treasury head Charles Trevelyan in August 1846. The government set up public works to provide wages, paltry as they proved to be, for potato farmers, but, as Woodham-Smith writes, "the provision of food for Ireland was to be left entirely to private enterprise and private traders." Not good enough.

Today the United States is far more enlightened on aid and trade as they affect hungry people than were the British in the 1840s. But we need political will to overcome crippling ideology and activate sound economic policies and development assistance that can make history out of world hunger. Let the devout among us say, St. Patrick, pray for us!

53. Imagine Your Grandfather's Hands

I was asked to deliver the invocation on March 17, 2007, at the annual dinner of the Friendly Sons of St. Patrick in Philadelphia. Nothing unusual about that, except for the fact that in Philadelphia, unlike other cities where I've gathered with the Friendly Sons, the friendly daughters were also present, along with bagpipers and young step-dancers.

One year earlier on that same evening in Scranton, Pennsylvania, I heard then mayor of Baltimore, now governor of Maryland, Martin O'Malley, address the all-male, eleven hundred strong, Lackawanna County chapter of the Friendly Sons. During his speech, Mr. O'Malley asked his hearers to open their hands in front of them and to notice the absence of scars, and dirt, and calluses there.

"Now," said this Irish American politician, "look through your hands and see the hands of your grandfathers and great grandfathers, the ones who dug the coal in this region, those who worked on the railroads and in the iron-works picking up the scars, dirt, and calluses along the way, even losing an occasional finger or two. And think of what they handed on to you—the gift of life and the faith, solid family values, educational opportunities. So be grateful tonight for them."

It was a powerful moment.

The audience had been doing remote preparation for that dinner beginning with luncheon libations that continued through the afternoon and into the evening. So they were understandably frisky and noisy when their dinner speaker began his address. But the rhetorical device of inviting the Friendly Sons to look through their hands and see their grandfathers brought the room to a hush.

I decided to highjack Martin O'Malley's idea for my invocation in Philadelphia on St. Patrick's night. I had nothing written out; I simply began by referring to the hands of all present and directing their reflection through those hands to the hands of their forebearers. As I did, I realized that there were women present, as indeed there were women—their grandmothers and great grandmothers—in the waves of immigration from Ireland to the United States more than a century ago. Once on our shores those hands turned to domestic service and washerwoman chores. So I included the work-worn hands of grandmothers in framing the invocation.

It worked. One person in that gathering wrote to me a few weeks later, "Each day since the dinner I look at my hands and recall your words relating to my father and mother coming to this land of opportunity, their contribution to building this great nation by sweat and toil." I received many requests for copies of the unwritten invocation.

One of the Philadelphia Friendly Sons sent me a copy of the Irish song, "Emigrant Eyes." He highlighted lyrics that refer to a clear-eyed young Irish emigrant who later became the singer's grandfather. In the song, the singer tells how he now looks into his grandfather's still clear "emigrant eyes" that seem to be looking back over a life of hard work and telling his grandson not to take success for granted.

None of us can afford to take for granted what our forebearers gave us. There are signs, however, that many in this nation of immigrants are now, several generations later, being pulled under by the quicksand of materialism and affluence, and losing both sight and sensitivity for those now knocking on our door. There is also evidence that the sons are forgetting what their fathers and grandfathers (many of them "Irish pols") did through the political process to build a better life in this land of opportunity for the unwashed and unwanted whose surnames now adorn our suburban mailboxes and downtown office directories.

54. A Principled Approach to Health Care Finance Reform

Everyone's looking for affordable health care. Too few of us are sufficiently outraged to do anything for roughly forty-five million of our fellow citizens who have no health insurance. That statistic offends the common good, but we lack the political will to do anything about it.

Analyzing this problem may be the first step toward nudging the nation toward a national health care policy that is comprehensive, efficient, effective, and fair. Those whose employment-related health insurance keeps them trapped in jobs or careers they'd prefer to shed for other career options but don't, because they can't risk losing their health insurance, might be helping themselves by giving some thought now to how the nation might provide health care security for all the uninsured, regardless of employment status.

Clear thinking on this question begins with precise vocabulary. Health care *finance* reform is the issue. With all its flaws, our health care *provision* capability is still arguably the best in the world, although some would dispute that. But its cost as a percentage of gross domestic product is too high. The cost of insurance coverage for those who will need health care is completely out of reach for many Americans and an excessive burden for millions more.

Reform must target both cost and coverage. There is no need, by and large, to worry about reforming the institutions and persons who are "providers," except to maintain private and public diligence on matters of medical and nursing education; credentialing and licensing; accreditation and patient safety; patient rights and provider compensation. None of these areas is problem free, but these problems do not call for radical reform, as does the twin problem of cost and coverage. Hence the importance of keeping the policy argument fixed on health care *finance* reform.

Coverage today is a spread of Medicare for the elderly, Medicaid for the poor or disabled, CHIP (Children's Health Insurance Program) for children, the Veteran's Administration for veterans of military service, and private insurance that is largely employment-based.

The millions who are uninsured are not included in any of these programs. For those who are included, coverage is uneven, prescription drugs are often not covered, and the costs are climbing.

Emergency room care is surely not the solution. Nor is uncompensated care through the charity of responsible providers. Justice, not charity, must drive the national response to this challenge. It's time to identify the justice ideals on which principled decisions about health care finance reform can be made.

Dick Davidson, when president of the American Hospital Association (AHA), had a point of view on all this. In a personal conversation with me, he said "we have a terribly broken payment system" and listed some principles that should be considered in repairing it. He believes "essential health services should be available to every American regardless of where they live or what they have in their pockets." The former AHA chief thinks everyone has a right to "timely access to the right care at the right time and in the right place." "The care provided," says Davidson, "should be safe, innovative, and coordinated, and it should be affordable." "No citizen or family should become impoverished because of medical expenses."

The only route to a solution, in my view, is federally financed, Medicare-like, basic coverage for every citizen, allowing for enhancements through private insurance by those individuals and employers who can afford it. Match this up against a federally monitored fee-for-service payment system and we will, I believe, be on the way to necessary health care finance reform.

Paying for it is an as-yet-unanswered question of political will. Some reform will happen on President Obama's watch; more will follow in the form of incremental changes over the years.

PART SEVEN

Purpose

55. Bring on the Individuarians

There is no room for individualism in Catholic social teaching, I once remarked in conversation with a Jewish friend. She thought there should be and wondered why I thought differently.

I explained that any "ism" throws a noun into italics, so to speak, or gives it a bold-faced emphasis that almost always results in an imbalance. Racism, sexism, and materialism are just three examples that I offered to make my point. I indicated that the word I've come up with to describe an individual who is unique, autonomous, and socially responsible is *individuarian*. The word is not in the dictionary, I acknowledged, but it is one that is useful to describe persons who are neither rugged individualists nor ideological communists, even though they are strong-minded individuals.

A good description of the wrong kind of individualist is offered by Mary Douglas and Steven Ney in a book called *Missing Persons*.

> Individualists, as the name implies, are not trying to create a community but rather aiming to free themselves from the fetters of social restriction. They thrive in loose organizational structures,

around which they can move freely without long-term commitment, able to negotiate their own dealings with other individuals. Well being for them means the freedom to pursue self-interested ends. It is the well being of the narrowly defined ego, the ideal of negative freedom from interference. (*Missing Persons*, Berkeley: University of California Press, 1998, p. 122)

We certainly don't need more of that in contemporary society. We need persons with higher ideals, larger hearts, wider horizons, and a positive sense of purpose. In searching for a label for this kind of person, I recalled that *communitarian* came into currency some years ago to describe a community-minded, socially responsible, environmentally sensitive, resourceful, and self-starting citizen. Might not individuarian be a good label now for the innovators and enablers we need to offset the community-eroding effects of individualism in daily life? Individuarians are needed now if America is to find a balanced future free of individualistic excesses.

The meaning of individualism, David Riesman wrote decades ago, depends on the historical setting. In America at mid-twentieth century, he saw newer varieties of what he labeled "groupism" becoming "increasingly menacing," while there was a corresponding rise in a character orientation he called "inner-direction" that was guided by values and ideals that made the principled persons who held them "appear to be more individualistic than they actually were." The "appear to be" qualifier is important.

I use individuarian to describe a good form of individualism. It is needed now, I think, to protect the common good from the extremes of self-centeredness on the right, or mindless groupism on the left. It serves to classify the strong individual who is intent on contributing to a stronger and measurably more just society by protecting and advancing the common good. Although respectful of competition and fully capable of confrontation, the individuarian prefers cooperation as an instrument of change on the way to community improvement.

I've written about this in a book called *Individuarian Observations*. It attempts to bring Catholic social reflection to bear on some of the issues that are often debated in the public policy arena.

We need more individuarians at all levels of society, if society itself is going to survive.

56. Are You Your Own Worst Enemy?

Charles Watson is professor of management at Miami University of Ohio. He and I have never met although we've talked on the phone and exchanged books and articles that each of us has authored. If we were in our early teens, we would be what they used to call "pen pals." As adult academics, we are kindred spirits interested in the formation of character and the restoration of integrity through education for business.

Are You Your Own Worst Enemy? is a book co-authored by Charles Watson and Thomas Indinopulos, a professor of comparative religions at Miami of Ohio. Knowing that I was on leave from a business school professorship to serve as president for two years of my high school alma mater, St. Joseph's Prep in Philadelphia, Charles Watson sent me a copy of his book along with a note saying, "Perhaps there are useful lessons here for your boys." Indeed there are.

Many if not most adolescents are, I've found, their own "worst enemy." They think the other kids are okay, but they are born to lose; they are not "with it," certainly not "cool." What they need is more encouragement and praise, along with the occasional and indispensable kick in the butt, to help them get themselves in gear to move forward in meeting life's challenges. They are, of course, our future, so strategies aimed at overcoming yourself-as-your-own-worst-enemy are solutions that all of us elders should be posting for their consideration. I did just that at the opening assembly of the St. Joseph's Prep student body in my second September as president there.

The subtitle of the Watson-Indinopulos book is "The Nine Inner Strengths You Need to Overcome Self-Defeating Tendencies at Work." I pointed out that they can be applied as well "at school" and I used the chapter headings as an outline for my talk to high school boys. Here's the list taken directly from the table of contents:

1. Develop What It Takes to Make Things Happen. Assume Responsibility, Initiate Action, Accept the Consequences.
2. Make the Most of Who You Are. Understand Yourself, Accept Yourself, Be Yourself.
3. Sharpen Your Thinking Skills. See beyond the Obvious, Pay Attention to Your Surroundings, Anticipate Consequences and Outcomes.
4. Be the Kind of Person Others Want to Be Around. Value Feelings, Treat Others with Dignity, Be an Encourager.
5. Break the Chains of Mindless Routine. Exercise Your Imagination, Turn Failures and Mistakes into Lessons, Rise above Mediocrity.

6. Become an Effective Learner and Continue Learning. Be Curious, Reflect on Your Observations, Expose Your Mind to New Ideas.
7. Master the Art of Self-Discipline. Assess Your Actions Honestly, Cause Your Emotions to Work for You, Learn to Make Favorable Impressions.
8. Act with Integrity. Know Good from Evil, Right from Wrong, Defeat Self-Centeredness, Pursue the Good and Right Wholeheartedly.
9. Be of Service to Others. Rise above Indifference, Have an Ultimate Concern That Goes Beyond Yourself, Serve Others Generously.

The authors say, "We wrote this book to show smart, capable, well-meaning people how their inner tendencies often lead to certain actions that make them into their own worst enemies" (*Are You Your Own Worst Enemy?* Westport, CT: Praeger, 2007, p. vii). I recommend the book with enthusiasm to those who want to see improvement in their workplace lives. If any of them are parents, they can use *Are You Your Own Worst Enemy?* as a playbook to help their youngsters put better numbers on their academic scoreboards while making progress on their own preparation for productive citizenship in the not too distant future.

Anyone who is at all interested in a fresh start in the pursuit of purpose in his or her life can use that table of contents as a practical examination of purpose, or employ it as a checklist to take a reading on the extent to which they are growing or declining in their quest to become fuller human beings.

57. A Lesson Plan for Life

Phil Martelli, the colorful, clever, and charismatic head basketball coach at St. Joseph's University in Philadelphia has written a book titled *Don't Call Me Coach: A Lesson Plan for Life*.

Why not call him coach, as John Wooden, UCLA's legendary basketball mentor, chose to be identified in his successful book, *They Call Me Coach*? Because Coach Martelli thinks "we are all coaches" and he wants to have a "conversation" with the rest of us. He does not view his "chosen profession as coaching, I'm a teacher," he says. "The court is my classroom."

According to Phil Martelli, "Successful coaching, like success in any other setting, is all about building relationships. It's about being organized and energizing people. A lot of coaching comes down to maximizing people's skills. And so...just about everyone who reads this book is a coach. Everyone who reads it is on a team [a family, business, school, charity, church]." There is not one of us "who doesn't build relationships, doesn't organize, energize, maximize the people and the skills and the tools that they have around them" (*Don't Call Me Coach: A Lesson Plan for Life*, Philadelphia: Camino Books, p. 2). The question, of course, is how well do we do this? Hence, Martelli's "lesson plan for life."

Before getting to that, however, the reader is introduced to a genuine Philly Cheese Steak experience of growing up as a "Philly guy" in a sports-obsessed city of well-defined neighborhoods, good schools, great families, and fierce loyalties. Phillies, Eagles, and Flyers fans divide their collegiate basketball loyalties unevenly among Penn's Quakers,

Temple's Owls, LaSalle's Explorers, Villanova's Wildcats, the recently emerging Drexel Dragons, and the St. Joseph's University Hawks with their crimson and gray conviction that "The Hawk Will Never Die!" Lucky for him, says Martelli, he managed to marry a "Philly girl," Judy Marra, who played her college basketball as a "Mighty Mac" at Immaculata in suburban Philadelphia.

"In coaching at any level," writes Martelli, "temperament is more important than technique." Taking a page from John Wooden's book, he acknowledges that "failing to prepare is preparing to fail." So he offers a three-P formula for doing well in any job: "preparation, not losing your perspective, and not prejudging others."

The launch pad for this book is the Hawks' thirty wins and two losses season of 2003–04. Martelli was college basketball's coach of the year. His team was ranked number one nationally when they hit the regular season twenty-seven win, no loss mark. His All-American point guard Jameer Nelson said it all after a last-second loss to Oklahoma State that barred the high-flying Hawks from entry to the NCAA Final Four: "My only goal was to be the best teammate anybody ever had. So because of that I know we didn't lose today."

Here are "Ten to Take with You"—principles that teacher Martelli wants all the rest of us coaches to remember:

All wins are not winning experiences; all losses are not losing experiences.

To get respect, you must first give it.

Every day be willing to teach; each day be open to learning.

The success of a group assures the success of an individual; it is never the other way around.

Don't take yourself too seriously.

Who you are is more important than what you do.

We have no more right to someone's time than we do to their money.

The eyes speak for the heart.

In all that you do, work (and play) hard, smart, and together.

Never let others know if you are working or playing; make it seem that you are doing both at the same time.

There's a good lesson plan for any life on or off the court.

58. The Shield of Shame

Could it be that we suffer from a serious shortage of shame in the world today? Whether they are shedding spouses in order to "find themselves," or shedding clothing with an eye to titillation and sexual attraction, otherwise "respectable" people either do, or gleefully observe, others doing outrageous things.

The whole world now knows that shame was no shield for Catholic priests and bishops who brought harm to children and disgrace to the Church. Ethical standards that hoodlums would regard as embarrassingly low pass as guidelines for right conduct in many corners of the American business system. Shred the documents. Bend the truth. Pocket the profits.

Human dignity—what's that? We live in something of a throwaway society and we now notice that people, even children, are being thrown away along with all our other trash. Have we no shame?

Language that would make a sailor blush is heard in the corridors of middle schools. Where's the shame?

A tracer can be put on the trail of disappearing shame by looking through the lens of embarrassment. Evidence of the disappearance of embarrassment among the young ranges over a wide field marked off by late arrivals for appointments (no apology), no thank-you notes (who says you have to do that?), fake IDs (drinking laws are silly), binge drinking (it eases stress), premarital sex (it feels good), cohabitation (everybody's doing it), abortion (I'm not ready for a child), drug abuse (I'm bored), theft (I'm only doing it to get by), infidelity (I'm weak), and on and on it goes through all age cohorts and class differences. It is not the wrong conduct or moral lapses that are remarkable; it is the willingness to be publicly identified with the conduct that prompts one to ask: Whatever became of shame?

Shame is linked with humiliation in human experience. It is an affect, a feeling. Shame is subject to rational control and it can be reasoned away as one comes to understand that this feeling of humiliation has no right to permanent residency in one's life. It can also be "rationalized" away in the sense of convincing oneself that there is no basis at all for feeling ashamed. Some of us elders have shown the young the way in this regard.

The rationalization machine can bend the mind into thinking that just about any vice is in fact a virtue, something to be proud of! Or, one can simply become desensitized to that which should and will, in normal circumstances, cause a person to feel shame—to be ashamed. The feeling is there for a purpose. Like fear, shame has a warning function; it exercises a protective role.

If society wants to protect its members, old and young, from the consequences of drug and alcohol abuse, theft and fraud, sexual promiscuity and related misconduct, from hurtful behavior of any kind, it must find ways to reintroduce the shield of shame in human affairs. This means being willing, as a society, to take a stand, to draw some lines. What's become of standards of good taste in entertainment, of fairness in business, and of professional integrity (including, sad to say, in the ranks of clergy who are supposed to be setting the standards)?

What we do in secret is a disclosure of our character. Shame can serve to tutor and strengthen character so that what one would not, because of good character, do in secret will not be done in public. Shame is a sentinel that should be on duty all the time.

Shame has a purpose that must not be ignored.

59. There Is Strength in Gentleness

On West Street at the edge of Shenandoah, Pennsylvania, there's an empty lot with a permanent marker that reads: "Site of the Birthplace and Boyhood Home of Walter J. Ciszek, SJ." Jesuit Father Walter Ciszek's 1964 book, *With God in Russia*, recounts the story of his growing up in Shenandoah; his leaving town in 1928, against his coal-miner father's will, to join the Jesuits; his post-ordination assignment to the "Russian Missions"; and his twenty-three years in Soviet prisons and labor camps for the crime of being a "Vatican spy."

My mother grew up, a little before him, just a few blocks from Wally Ciszek's birthplace. Her father was the town's "general physician and surgeon." He delivered most of the babies and attended, my mother once told me, to the victims of violence in the days of the Molly Maguire labor uprisings in the coalfields. Her family home on Main Street, which housed my grandfather's office, was, like the Ciszek home, eventually razed. There is no historic marker there now, just a gas station and convenience store.

I have many memories of childhood visits to Shenandoah. Sunday morning bells called worshipers to the "Irish" church (the official Catholic diocesan parish), the Lithuanian church, the Italian church, the Polish church, and several onion-dome Greek churches. There were a few Protestant churches in town and a synagogue, too.

The "Pool," a weekly lottery, brought everyone into town for lively Saturday nights. Some residents called the borough "little New York." Located midway between Scranton and Harrisburg just off Interstate 81, Shenandoah had a population of about twenty-five thousand when anthracite was king; it's down to fifty-six hundred now. Hispanics, mostly Mexicans, attracted by factory work and farm labor opportunities, have added to the ethnic mix.

I have memories of seeing tough little kids like Wally Ciszek (whom I didn't know then but met many years later) smoking cigars. One of my cousins, Tom Coakley, played football for Shenandoah High. I had the impression from him that the gridiron surface was more coal slag than grass. They were all tough kids in the 1920s and '30s in Shenandoah.

Sadly, Shenandoah is now making disturbing national news. On July 14, 2008, Luis Ramirez, age twenty-five, an illegal Mexican immigrant, died from head injuries and a severe beating at the hands of several teenage boys, all Shenandoah High School football players. They are of Slovak, Irish, Lithuanian, and Polish extraction. They are probably Catholic and I'd be willing to bet that they received their elementary education in the town's consolidated Catholic school that bears the name of Walter J. Ciszek, SJ. Their motive in killing Ramirez, according to the *New York Times*, is not altogether clear, but ethnic tensions and hatred, fueled by alcohol, appear to be the cause.

Many of my relatives are buried in the Annunciation Cemetery in Shenandoah Heights, overlooking the town. I visit there once or twice a year. I have no living relatives in town now so when I return, I typically see familiar places but no one that I know. Ethnic diversity is nothing new; the hatred, however, is.

Ironically, in a summer of ethnic violence in a tiny town connected to the rest of the world by television, residents of Shenandoah must know that *South Pacific* has returned to Broadway after a fifty-year absence. I hope they'll hear the song from that show that reminds us, "You've got to be taught to hate." Who taught these Shenandoah teenagers to hate?

As high school football gets up and running again all over the country every fall, who's going to convince the athletes that playing hard is okay, but playing dirty isn't; that strength is good, but violence bad; that life within the rules is the good life, and that success on the field must never yield to arrogance on the streets?

We have to demonstrate to our young the wisdom of strength-in-gentleness, and teach them there is no place for hatred in their lives. Wally Ciszek, pray for us.

60. Keeping Kids Free of Drugs

The entire full-page ad is worth repeating. There it was in the *New York Times*, October 1, 2004, page A17:

How to Keep Your Kids Free of Drugs
Rule #1.
Understand Why.
Almost always, it's rebellion, alienation, despair,
peer pressure, or some combination.
As a parent you can always have a powerful effect on
how your kids deal with these things.
And whether they see drugs as an answer. One of the
biggest deterrents is talking with your kids about drugs.
To learn more, call for a free parent's handbook.
1-800-729-6686
Partnership for a Drug-Free America
www.drugfreeamerica.org

I went to the Web site and what did I find? Lots of helpful information, to be sure, but I was not successful in getting to why, in understanding Rule #1, in tracking down the reason, in cornering the culprit hidden behind that one word, *why*. Why do kids do drugs?

That's a demand-side question. Typically the "war on drugs" is fought on the supply side—going after the dealers, burning the poppy fields, capturing the supply—but if there were no demand there would be no market to supply. The question of why remains. Why do kids use drugs?

I think that deep down on the demand side of the problem of drug abuse in America lie three causal considerations. First is the desire—known to every healthy, normal person—to experience the exhilaration of a "high." Drug-induced highs, however, bring with them a dependency on drugs. Highs resulting from athletic, academic, artistic, or other achievements associated with plain hard work are unaccompanied by destructive dependencies, but they don't come easily.

The second causal consideration is the desire to avoid pain—physical or psychological pain. Pain has no redemptive value in a secular society. Avoidance of all pain, at all times, by any means, is a supreme value. Our cultural denigration of pain, disappointment, discouragement, and monotony encourages escape at any price. Creativity can overcome boredom, but creativity does not come easily.

The third causal consideration in examining the why behind the demand for drugs, as I see it, is biological. Babies born of addicted mothers are themselves addicts. Other biological predispositions are possible, but they won't become addictions if addictive substances are never used. However, refusal to use drugs does not come easily for many, especially when "everyone's doing it."

There are other reasons why. Some people just like to take risks. But where addictive substances are involved, risk takers rarely recognize that there is not risk, but virtual certainty that one experience can lead to the captivity of addiction—not cause it immediately, but lead to it inevitably. Risk taking is as easy as ignorance.

If you want to keep your kids free from drugs, I would suggest that you help them not be taken in by the big lie our culture of consumerism perpetuates. Kids have to be helped to understand that to have is not to be, that to have more is not necessarily to be more, and that to live easily is not the route to living happily.

Since what you do speaks a lot louder than what you say, first check yourself out on those consumerism counts and then have something clear and convincing to say to your kids about the easy life never being the road to happiness.

61. The Other Fellow First

For the past twenty or so summers, I've spent a long week-end at Camp Dudley on Lake Champlain in Westport, New York. Dudley is the oldest continuous summer camp for boys in the United States. It was founded by the Young Men's Christian Association in 1884 and although no longer under YMCA sponsorship, maintains a nondenominational commitment to Christian values while operating under an independent self-perpetuating governing board.

I think of Camp Dudley whenever asked to explain the meaning of the word *culture*. A culture, as the late Canadian Jesuit theologian Bernard Lonergan once said, "is a set of meanings and values informing a common way of life, and there are as many cultures as there are distinct sets of such meanings and values."

Any culture is defined by a dominant and shared value. There is an identifiable Wall Street culture, a youth culture, a culture of violence, an ecclesiastical culture, and many artistic "cultural societies." At Camp Dudley, the dominant value that shapes the culture is articulated in the camp's motto: "The Other Fellow First."

Ministers of various Christian denominations conduct the Sunday noon "chapel service" each week at Camp Dudley.

Sitting on timbers lodged into a slope bordered by tall pine trees that stretch down toward the lake, campers have to wear a shirt, tie, and blazer above an interesting variety of chino and khaki pants, short or long, as they say and sing their praise and thanks to God. (The Catholic campers are taken to mass in nearby Westport on Saturday afternoon or early Sunday morning, but are back in time for the ecumenical Sunday service.) One Sunday I preached to this camper congregation on the Gospel story of the Good Samaritan and asked, as I began, "By the way, what's the Dudley motto?" Their voices rang out, "The other fellow first," and that response, of course, set me up to make the homiletic point I had in mind.

One year, my annual visit happened to coincide with Parents Weekend. I was chatting with a man and wife whose eight-year-old son was a first-time camper. The youngster was not present when his parents told me that they lived on the Upper East Side of New York City and that their boy attended a select (some would say "posh") private school where he had a few "adjustment problems." Soon the boy approached us. He waddled more than walked. He was overweight and showed signs of underconfidence. My ice-breaker question, "What do you like most about Camp Dudley," drew an answer that told me the Dudley culture was working well: "Nobody here makes fun of you."

Jesuit schools around the world have been getting a lot of mileage for the past couple of decades from the slogan that captures the essence of their educational mission: to educate "men and women for others." More than one Jesuit high school parent has heard the dinner-table comment of an oppressed sibling to an older brother, "Hey, you're supposed to be a man for others. How about me?" A great ideal has taken hold. Slogans help.

Before the lights go out each night in every Camp Dudley cabin, the boys and their "Leader" have "Vespers." This is not liturgical prayer. It is instead story time. The narrative focuses on values. Over time, the values become internalized principles.

The Dudley motto was embodied in the person of the late Willie Schmidt, who ran the camp when I first went there in the 1980s. Willie and his wife Lois made Dudley great. Keeping the place great today is Andy Bisselle, a long-time camper, later leader, and now director. Andy and his wife Fran built their own happy marriage on the principle of "the other fellow first." Countless happy lives, marriages, and careers are rooted in that same bedrock principle, which is alive and well today at Dudley.

And when Andy is asked to explain the rationale for the activity-packed agenda of camp events, he often describes the program as, "Fun with a purpose."

62. Self-Service in Pursuit of a New Career

"Losing a job after giving yourself so totally to one organization is like getting cancer," said a veteran of twenty years as director of personnel in a large publishing company. With no notice, he was on the street, "truly frightened that I would never find another suitable job," he told me. "You know perfectly well on one level it can happen and you try to prepare yourself, but the reality is so totally stunning it's like walking into a steel beam in the dark." It took him eight months to find comparable employment in another industry in the same metropolitan area. He credits "a marvelous outplacement counselor" with "saving" him. That person "put the old starch back in me and restored my faith in myself. Alternating between stroking my ego and kicking my butt, he instilled in me the belief that I would find another job and a good one, and he was right."

Waves of layoffs hit the American economy every ten years or so. Everyone seems to know someone who had been "downsized," "re-engineered," ground under by the wheels of corporate "restructuring." Machine-tool metaphors are often used to mute or mask the painful impact of job loss on hurting human beings. With the loss of job all too often there seems to be a loss of purpose.

Common sense suggests that you have a self to serve during the transition from one job to another. You are your sole client, your chief concern. Throughout the transition, you are the center of a process of personal self-assessment and self-renewal; you must be or become the object of your own self-esteem and self-respect. You are the one who has to guard against self-pity, loss of self-confidence. You are the agent of change. If new employment is to be found, you have to take the initiative. The process is fundamentally self-serving, and there is absolutely nothing to apologize for in acknowledging that it is. Ultimately, the job search is a test of character, and character, as both history and literature attest, is proved in action.

If you happen to be in transition—"between engagements" as unemployed actors would say—you have to recognize that you are both the product and the sales force in your personal job campaign. You are the "corpus" to be moved from here to there; you are the "corporation" that does the moving. Getting to know the product is, not surprisingly, an indispensable first step toward making this important sale—the reconnection of yourself with meaningful employment. Your return trip to full employment should begin this way. First, demand of yourself an honest answer to the question of who you are. Not what you do or want to do, but who you are. What are your values, the nonnegotiables in your life? Then ask what you want to do. What line of work best matches up with your basic values?

I wrote a book about this in 1995. It is now out of print. Since layoffs are back in the headlines and mid-career job seekers are on the rise, you can, if you are so inclined, type the title—*Finding Work without Losing Heart*—into your search engine and you might be able to find a copy. It has pumped purpose back into the hearts of discouraged job seekers. Search it out and give it a try.

63. The Paradox of Our Times

When I was pastor at Holy Trinity in Georgetown, I invited a Benedictine Abbot, Aidan Shea, to administer the sacrament of confirmation to our young adults. He incorporated into his confirmation homily a reflection that caught the interest of many parishioners. I received many requests for a copy of that reflection. Abbot Shea had mentioned that he thought the words came from an article he had read in *The New Yorker*, but he didn't have an exact citation. He later indicated that he couldn't remember exactly where he first ran across the words he quoted. So I did an Internet search and found that the quotation has appeared in many places, including an Ann Landers column. A notation by the great editor-in-chief of those quotation pages that float around out there in cyberspace indicates simply, "author unknown."

It seems so timely now, given what is happening in the world around us. I'll post it here without attribution of authorship, because the author remains, to me at least, unknown.

> The paradox of our times is that we have taller buildings, but shorter tempers; wider freeways, but narrower viewpoints. We buy more, but enjoy it less.
>
> We have bigger houses and smaller families; more conveniences, but less time; we have more advanced degrees, but less common sense; more knowledge, but less good judgment; more medicine, but less wellness.
>
> We have multiplied our possessions, but reduced our values. We have higher incomes, but lower morals.
>
> We have been all the way to the moon and back, but have trouble crossing the street to meet a new neighbor. We've conquered outer space, but inner space is still a mystery to too many of us.
>
> We have cleaned up the air, but polluted the soul; we have split the atom, but not our prejudices.
>
> It is a time when there is much in the show window and nothing in the stockroom; a time when technology can bring a letter to you in seconds, and you can choose whether to make a difference or just hit "delete."

Before all those family and personal resolutions we always seem to be making relating to temper, time management, wellness, higher morals, love of neighbor, self-control, and prejudice fade from consciousness, it would surely be wise to post that text on the fridge or frame it on the wall for further reflection.

Who knows what wisdom might emerge from a family competition to add a paradox or two to the list? Declare an open season each year for new entries through the forty days of Lent and pick the winner on Easter Sunday.

Parents and grandparents can look back through the shelves of memory to find paradoxical situations. The youngsters can create their own or consult the anthologies for well-turned phrases from the past. The point of it all is to widen our awareness of the things to which we should be attending, and the risk we run of inattention to old values that are becoming candidates for inclusion on an endangered species list as a sense of personal and national purpose slips away.

PART EIGHT
Education

64. September and the Joy of Teaching

Some would say that there's no better place in the world to work than on a college campus in the month of September. The same could probably be said of elementary and secondary school settings. All educators know how good it is to return after the summer break.

In September, everyone is refreshed and ready to go. Old friends reconnect; new friendships are ready to be made. On college campuses student newcomers are only four years out of the eighth grade—not so intimidating as they may appear.

In September, no college team has had a losing season yet. No student has flunked a course yet. No faculty member has been denied a raise or promotion yet. Although some may not have a parking space right next to the building where they teach, and others may have experienced bookstore glitches, most faculty are happy, content, and grateful to be engaged in the privileged work of contributing to the development of human potential.

If only the September glow could run straight through to March, it would be paradise!

Thoreau once remarked that "most men lead lives of quiet desperation." (If he were writing today, he might also include women in that assessment.) Even if you disagree with his "most" quantification, you will have noticed, if you spend any time at all on a college campus, that more than a few of the folk Thoreau had in mind seem to wind up on college and university faculties. Too bad that these few don't catch the spirit of service and share the deep sense of vocation that add meaning to the lives of so many faculty professionals. They have something that no amount of money or acclaim could give them. It has to make you wonder when those long winters of campus discontent set in, how professors whose teaching enriches the lives of others can let the life of their own minds just go flat.

The great American Church historian Monsignor John Tracy Ellis reserved his severest criticism for faculty colleagues who "simply stopped reading; they don't read anymore." His friend, Monsignor George Higgins, the expert on Catholic social thought who specialized in labor issues, once remarked to Ellis and me, "I've never been bored a day in my life. How can anyone be bored when there are so many books yet to be read?"

If your September reflections bring back good memories of student days, take a moment to send a note of appreciation to teachers and other guides who made those days memorable. Think now of ways in which you might assist classroom teachers to supplement their income by consulting during the year and, if they want to, taking on vacation projects for pay in the summer months. Do all you can to prevent educational pay levels from falling too low. Money is not the only thing, but it is not an unimportant consideration in attracting and holding good teachers to the classroom.

All of us, regardless of where we work and what we do, can find help in fending off the demon of "quiet desperation" by reading John Gardner's small classic *Self Renewal*. He ends the book on this note: "One may not quite accept Oliver Wendell Holmes' dictum—'Every calling is great when greatly pursued'—but the grain of truth is there." That's a truth most educators gladly recommit themselves to every September.

65. Catholic Mission and Identity

There is a lot of conversation these days about Catholic identity in Catholic schools, colleges, and hospitals. I've been interested in that topic over the years because of administrative responsibilities in Catholic higher education. But when I became president of my high school alma mater, St. Joseph's Prep in Philadelphia, in 2006, I began looking at the mission and identity question through the secondary school lens.

The admissions brochure stated that "the mission of St. Joseph's Prep as a Catholic, Jesuit, urban, college preparatory school is to develop the minds, hearts, souls, and characters of young men in their pursuit of becoming men for and with others." We decided to engage students, faculty, alumni, trustees, and others in spelling out what is meant by each of those four defining characteristics.

I'll touch on just one of them here—the Catholic marker.

In defining what we mean by "Catholic," we said that the school "is grounded in the person and teachings of Jesus Christ who established a Church that has a tradition, creed, body of doctrine, moral code, and sacramental system that are essential to the life and culture of this school." It is helpful, of course, to say, as that sentence does, what we mean by "Catholic," but more important to say what we do because we are Catholic. Here are five *quia clauses* (*quia* is the Latin word for *because*) that spell out the educational consequences of our Catholic commitment. We incorporated these into our mission statement:

> Because we are Catholic, "we strive for a personal relationship of friendship with Jesus Christ so that we may, in the words of St. Ignatius Loyola, founder of the Jesuit order that sponsors this school, 'love him more intensely and follow him more closely.'"

> Because we are Catholic, "instruction and formation in religion, rooted in both Scripture and Tradition, covers Catholic faith and morals while opening the minds of students to an ecumenical outlook and an appreciation of, and respect for, other faith traditions."

> Because we are Catholic, "we foster in students a consciousness of their shared sonship under God and their brotherhood with men and women of all races, nations, and cultures of the world."

> Because we are Catholic, "we instruct our students in their responsibilities as stewards of God's creation. Because we are Catholic, it is our aim to form leaders—men of competence, conscience, and compassionate commitment—who choose to order their lives in a radical way toward God, as modeled for us by Jesus Christ in love and service to others, all for the greater glory of God."

Similarly, we wrote into our mission statement what we mean by Jesuit, urban, and college preparatory, and go on to spell out the consequences for our school of each of those defining attributes. Anyone interested in reading what we claim can take a look at www.sjprep.org.

By specifying that we aim to educate "men for and with others" (we are an all-boys school), we incorporate into our mission statement the words of the late Superior General of the Jesuit Order, Father Pedro Arrupe, who said in 1973, "Today our prime educational objective must be to form men for others." Father Arrupe's successor, Father Peter Hans Kolvenbach, introduced the notion of "men with" as well as "for" others in order to make the point that those moved by Ignatian spirituality are in solidarity with those they help and can learn from them.

It is a healthy exercise for any institution to state its mission and then face up to the challenge of pursuing the implications of what that statement says. The *quia clauses* are, as the saying goes, the place where "the rubber hits the road."

66. Pick a Context Not a Campus

Every year hundreds of thousands of families find themselves looking at colleges in search of the right choice for a teenage son or daughter. The sons and daughters do a lot of looking on their own, of course, and all sorts of conversations, negotiations, and spirited arguments ensue before a firm decision is made.

Who decides? More often than not, the parents decide because they have to foot the bills. Not infrequently, grandparents get into the act, along with uncles, aunts, and high school advisers. Many parents have both the courage and wisdom to leave the final choice to the child who will have to live with the decision for a lifetime. But all too often the decision, whether made by the parents or their offspring, even though it may eventually prove to be "right," is made for the wrong reasons.

My years as a college professor, dean, and president have set me up for annual requests from friends for letters of recommendation as well as advice on where their children or grandchildren should apply. If given the opening, I'll always say, "Look at the context, not just the campus." Now what do I mean by that?

First, it is important to check out the campus culture. What are the dominant values that characterize, even permeate the campus and define the culture? How do those values match up with one's family values, religious values, and personal goals? Not to say that some cultural diversity is not good; it can and will add educational value to the collegiate years. But the question remains: Which values dominate?

A sound alignment between campus values and one's personal, family, and faith values will not just happen at many otherwise "good" schools. A student's potential for managing the value conflict has to be measured before the decision to enroll is made.

I also suggest that there is a high probability that one's future spouse will be met during the collegiate years. It is a virtual certainty that lifelong friendships will be formed with college classmates, so it is wise to look around to see what kind of a crowd you'll be hanging out with when you commit yourself to a particular school.

Check out the library, I always tell them. It is more important than the athletic complex or student center (just as in any good college all that is represented by the library card will be valued more than what is purchased by the credit card). Right ideas will always trump expensive possessions for graduates of really good colleges. Read what colleges have to say about themselves in their recruitment literature. If it is short on educational ideas and long on NCAA success stories, keep on looking.

My advice is not always heeded. But I offer it just to add a few extra branches to the decision tree.

Other factors, in addition to tuition and financial aid, have to be considered. Take location: Is an urban, suburban, or rural setting best for this particular student? Quality of faculty is surely important, but will faculty "stars" ever appear in undergraduate classrooms? Class size is worthy of consideration. A low classroom student-to-faculty ratio is a high program-quality indicator. Check median SAT scores of the last few freshman classes. A rising SAT tide lifts all academic boats. Technological infrastructure deserves a look. Is there a portal at every pillow? Finally, the brand name. Will the name of your alma mater enhance your job prospects after graduation?

Whenever a dreamy-eyed youngster says, "I fell in love with the campus the moment I saw it," the stage is set for a "learning moment" that begins with the question: What did you actually see? The choice of a lifetime deserves careful consideration of the wider context within which the most beautiful campus imaginable is just one of many interesting and intriguing parts.

67. Formula for Success in College

Any beginning, returning, or second-chance college student can find the key to academic success on a single $8\frac{1}{2}''$-by-$11''$ sheet of paper.

If you are a concerned parent, you can pack that sheet in with all the other gear your offspring will be carrying away to college. This sheet of paper is called a "study budget."

If you are a student, it is a paper to be filled in by you. If followed, it becomes a reliable roadmap to a college diploma. Here's how it works.

Take the sheet and draw vertical lines to produce seven columns; then draw horizontal lines to make twenty-four rows—one column for each of the seven days in every week, one row corresponding to each of the twenty-four hours of every day. Label them accordingly down the side and across the top of the page. An important point to note as you begin this project is that there may be other students in your class with higher IQs, fatter bank accounts, wider travel experience, and more impressive secondary school credentials than you have, but no one has more days in the week or hours in the day than you. When you construct a study budget, no one has a bigger sheet than yours—24/7 means equal opportunity for all!

Once you get your class schedule, fill in those blocks that correspond to class and lab time. That, of course, is time already taken; nothing you can do about it. Next, figure out how many blocks should be blackened out for sleep, meals, extracurriculars, and normal recreation. Then write the letter "S" into a sufficient number of the remaining blocks so that you will have set aside study time for each day beginning with Monday of the first full week of class. Now notice all the white space in the Saturday and Sunday columns and proceed to blacken out some weekend study hours so that they will be "taken," so to speak, and not available for frisbee flipping, televiewing, hanging out, or roaming off the reservation in response to impulse, invitation, or unanticipated opportunities that would pull you away from the books.

Then take a long minute to ponder the difference between a money-expenditure budget and a study budget. If you save up your money week by week, you'll surely have a lot to spend on a future blowout weekend with friends. But you can't save and accumulate study time. It has to be spent every day or it just won't be there to be spent at any future date. Understanding that simple truth admits you to the world of the wise.

Now, of course, you have to allow for spontaneity and make allowance for the unexpected. But remember, if you've squirreled your study time away by not spending it, you are in big trouble as early as three or four weeks into your first semester. An additional week or two with no expenditures from your study budget will put you in a hole so deep that you are unlikely ever to return to the land of the academic living.

Once your study budget is complete, take it to a duplicating machine and run off a few copies—one for the folks at home, one for the wall by your desk, and one for a good friend who cares enough about you to introduce you to your better self whenever you deviate from the plan. That's what a study budget is—a plan for academic success. The design-and-build responsibilities are all yours. So are the good results.

68. College Students and Respect for Human Dignity

I know of a professor in an elite business school who uses an unusual device to make his students more aware of the importance of recognizing the dignity of all persons in the workplace. In his mid-term exam, he asks: "Please list the name of the person who cleans this classroom every day." In response to the howls of protest and charges of unfairness that question always generates, he simply says: "Not unfair, because I'm telling you now that I will make it up to you by asking the same question on the final. You now have that question in advance of the test. And, by the way, if you don't have enough sensitivity to recognize that a real person with a real name works for you every day by putting this place into good shape for class, then you're going to fail as a boss in the real world of work by not noticing that you have real people with real dignity on your payroll who happen to be doing important but menial jobs."

News from the universities of Stanford and Georgetown about a decade ago served to reassure anyone wondering whether privileged college students have any concern for the welfare of the hired hands who keep their classrooms and residence halls clean. Students at Stanford organized the "Habla Program" to help immigrant campus workers, mostly Mexicans, learn English. Tutoring takes place in the student center where more than language learning happens; friendships are formed and burritos are shared.

At Georgetown, about twenty students went on a nine-day hunger strike for wage increases and improved benefits for contract workers. "Living Wage" read the sign over the mid-campus campground set up by the protestors who chose an admittedly controversial means to communicate their concerns to the administration. They were not exactly pushing against an open door, but the administration listened and responded positively.

Georgetown President John J. DeGioia approved an increase in total compensation for contract workers from a minimum of $11.33 an hour to thirteen dollars by July 2006, moving up to fourteen dollars by July 2007. According to the *Washington Post*, DeGioia sees the change, which affected about four hundred fifty contract janitors, food-service, and security workers, as "an appropriate next step for us" in the university's ongoing efforts to ensure good working conditions. He also remarked with a smile on the "irony" of the situation because he had taught some of the protestors in philosophy classes that dealt with human rights.

In a context unrelated to all of this, Robin Raskin, who describes herself as a "$300,000-plus-tuition-paying mom," wrote a letter to the editor of the *Atlantic Monthly* in December 2004 acknowledging that it's not unusual "for upper-middle-class parents to become apoplectic about the college-admissions process." She wondered why more are not concerned "about the kind of citizen that comes out the other side." Her letter was a response to an earlier article about connecting practical and traditional education. Here's one of several suggestions she offered to college administrators: "Lose the country-club motif. I don't mind my kids' having to learn to clean a toilet, plant a shrub, or paint their dorm (especially if it'll keep tuition costs down). Telling them that they can study while others pick up their garbage is something I'd never do at home. It's misguided and it makes for rotten citizens."

While admiring the social conscience of Georgetown hunger strikers and Stanford tutors, those providing higher education to student-citizens anywhere can do more. They should be thinking of ways to encourage civility, respect, courtesy, and cooperation, on the part of students, toward those who do their dirty work. Calling them by name is an easy first step.

69. Leaving Campus with a Diploma—and Integrity

In 1954, at the outdoor commencement on the Avenue of the Oaks on the beautiful Spring Hill College campus in Mobile, Alabama, a public announcement was made that Spring Hill would enroll African American students the following September. Racial integration came to the college the same year the U.S. Supreme Court announced its landmark "Brown vs. Board of Education" decision declaring state-mandated racial segregation in public schools unconstitutional.

In his famous 1963 letter from the Birmingham jail—an appeal to the conscience of white Church leadership in the South—the Rev. Dr. Martin Luther King Jr. had a word of praise for Spring Hill. He expressed disappointment over lack of white support in the struggle for civil rights for blacks, but, he said, "Some of our white brothers in the South have grasped the meaning of this social revolution and committed themselves to it."

He added, "I commend the Catholic leaders of this state [Alabama] for integrating Spring Hill College several years ago." It was nine years earlier that Spring Hill integrated over the opposition of many inside and outside the campus community.

I was there on the Avenue of the Oaks to deliver the commencement address to the class of 2004. I reminded them of the 1954 decision and asked them to think about integration and integrity in their personal lives.

These students knew all about racial integration and, to their credit, welcomed it and celebrated its presence. They wondered why it was such a big deal back in the '50s. They now have to consider other social justice issues that will challenge their personal commitment.

So I asked them to think about integration in their personal lives—integration of faith and reason, body and soul, matter and spirit, leisure and work, pleasure and pain. I invited them to notice the need in their lives for integration of so many good realities, all of them necessary for achieving the good life. They must "have it all together," as the saying goes, if they are going to lead genuinely happy and productive lives.

How to integrate family and work, idealism and realism, giving and receiving, gain and loss, sacrifice and satisfaction? These are all goods whose integration in one's personal life will build a balance of genuine reality—the reality through which all of us must walk on our journey to eternal fulfillment.

There is sometimes a hard edge to the reality that enters a human life. There is the reality of pain and illness, of loss and failure, of being wronged and hurt by others. The Christian approach to reality, summarized in the Paschal Mystery, prepares the believer to deal with reality's hard edge.

Just as graduating seniors measure themselves for caps and gowns before commencement, they should take a graduation moment to measure their own personal integrity. I told the Spring Hill graduates that I think of integrity in terms of wholeness, solidity of character, honesty, trustworthiness, responsibility. A person of integrity has a sense of self, knows where he or she stands. I invited them to carry with them a take-home exam on integrity along with their diplomas.

Those stately trees on the Avenue of the Oaks challenge the young to go their separate ways together in the tradition of integrity that is part of Spring Hill's history. People of great integrity are responsible for the racial integration there and elsewhere in America today—far from perfect, but lots of progress since 1954.

70. Growing Greatness at the Gesu School

Parents describe it as a "safe haven." Teachers call it a great place to work. The children—all four hundred fifty of them, boys and girls, preschool through eighth grade—arrive early, leave late, and want to be there every day. It is the Gesu, an independent Catholic school in North Central Philadelphia.

One day two preschool students were in the office of the head of the school. A family photograph on a shelf behind her desk prompted one of the children to ask: "Who are they?" "My family," she replied, and named them one by one. When she came to her father, she mentioned that he had died not long ago. "Did he get shot?" asked one of the four-year-olds.

Violence is more familiar to these youngsters than secure neighborhoods and stable families. Not surprisingly, then, one of the former teachers, who now sits on the sixty-one-member board of trustees, spoke up at a weekend board retreat in 2007 and said that the school is very good at "creating a safe haven that nurtures the whole person who then goes on to make a positive contribution to society." Well, they're not all there yet, but they are certainly on their way, as I learned while sitting in on that board retreat.

The school has origins in the Jesuit-run Gesu Parish, established in 1868, but suppressed by the Archdiocese of Philadelphia in 1993 in the face of rising costs and a sharply declining parishioner population. Father George Bur, the Jesuit pastor, accepted the decision to close the parish gracefully but immediately rallied lay suburbanite friends to save the school.

Since then, they have raised twenty million dollars (seven million dollars from Jewish philanthropists who recognize that "those kids have no constituency"). They have a thirteen-million-dollar endowment. Average faculty pay in 2008 was $41,500. Volunteer assistance is plentiful and highly skilled. There are twenty-nine full-time teachers and seven full-time aides.

The Gesu thrives today as a joint-venture of the Maryland Province Jesuits in partnership with the West Chester, Pennsylvania-based Sisters, Servants of the Immaculate Heart of Mary (IHMs). One IHM nun is the principal, another is a counselor. Two Jesuits are part of the team—one as a teacher and coach, the other as "prefect of discipline." Gesu is non-selective and open admissions, but 90 percent of the graduates finish high school, as compared with the 50 percent high-school graduation rate for other children from the same geographic area who go to public schools.

Board members, faculty, volunteers, and administrators spoke at the retreat of their "passion" for the school. Their aim is to instill in the children "hope and the courage to escape poverty, and violence, on their way to becoming life-long learners and leaders in the community."

The school affirms the culture of the children. It respects where they come from. "But we're going to make you masters of two cultures," says an African American male teacher; "we're going to give you the skills you need so that you can compete downtown."

The kids suffer from vacant vocabularies; their minds are imprisoned by verbal deficits. In a classroom discussion, no third-grader knew what a "rodeo" was. Many of the words they need to break free of limitations have never been heard at home, which is typically a single parent household headed by a female who struggles to get by on two or three jobs.

Gesu children get heavy doses of math and language arts. Religion is required too, although fewer than 10 percent are Catholic. Reading is emphasized. Greatness is growing at the Gesu, one child at a time.

71. Reflections on the Tragedy at Virginia Tech

Ever since the Columbine high school massacre in 1999 and the Washington, DC, Beltway sniper attacks of 2002, *lockdown* is a word that's been lifted out of the penitentiary lexicon and dropped into student handbooks across the nation.

When shots are heard, go immediately into a protective lock-down mode and await further instructions from authorities.

But how do you lock down a sprawling campus? How do you make hundreds of campus buildings, replete with entrances and exits, safe from armed attackers or hidden bombs? Is there any defense against malice and, if there is, how can you tell if and when it's coming?

It is malice, by the way, that was operative in the Beltway snipings, Columbine killings, and the April 16, 2007, Virginia Tech massacre. There is evil in the world. Malice can find its way into the minds and hearts of persons young or old. Once there, malicious intent can release destructive force. Two high school students killed twelve of their peers and a teacher and wounded twenty-four at Columbine, before taking their own lives. One gunman killed thirty-two and then himself at Virginia Tech. The suicide at Virginia Tech ended the search for a perpetrator but shed no light on the motive. We were left to wonder why, as we pondered prevention possibilities on campuses everywhere.

On what would have been an otherwise normal spring morning at Virginia Tech, a campus community of some twenty-six thousand was neither ready nor able to prevent the largest massacre in the history of American education. But was the campus community unprepared? To ask the same question in another way, was any preparation possible?

The campus community was not necessarily unprepared. Yes, preparation is indeed possible. In the Christian view of life-after-death, preparation for life-through-death is a definite possibility. Indeed it is a necessity for the success-ful completion of a Christian life.

Prevention, as opposed to preparation, neither is nor was possible at Virginia Tech. Why? Because there is no defense against malice in our world. But preparation is always possible. There is a preparation for anything in a person whose human will is aligned with the will of God. Preparation for any eventuality is the story of a human life lived in accord with the will of the Creator of that life.

That's why campus ministry is as important as the counseling center on a college campus. Certainly, psychological trauma requires immediate attention, but so does the stress on faith and the strain on spirituality. Moreover, the power of faith and religion to ready the human spirit to withstand any assault, physical or psychological, cannot be overestimated. That's why the Church has to provide this ministry in campus settings that are not Catholic.

Liturgically—especially sacramentally—the believer must be helped to heal in the broken places. Near-campus parishes and on-campus ministry centers provide the space and facilitate the reflection that students need if they are to permit sacramental grace and the interpretative framework provided by the Christian Gospel to work the wonders they are capable of working.

The physical attractiveness and proximity of Catholic ministry facilities to the students are important. The young must be drawn to them during their formative years so that they can reflect on the meaning of life, their purpose in life, and the laws of God within which the good life is to be lived.

Without ministry, we will be permitting our young to sleepwalk, at their peril, through a world of good and evil. Preparation is always possible even where prevention fails.

PART NINE

Business

72. Measuring Corporate Social Responsibility

Ideology can distort reality in discussions of the social responsibilities of business. Fear of being labeled "a liberal" can prompt business leaders to dismiss the notion of corporate social responsibility, even when they themselves act in socially responsible ways—protecting the environment, creating employment, supporting the arts and education. Fear of appearing friendly to capitalism can, on the other hand, blind the social reformer to the potential for good within the capitalist system.

I believe a humanistic capitalism is not only possible but desirable. I would reject both fatalism and revolution, while choosing reform, as the instrument of social change that is waiting to be applied to the circumstances that surround us today in the American economy. The fact of the matter is that far too many corporate citizens are not meeting their social responsibilities.

Archie B. Carroll described "The Pyramid of Corporate Social Responsibility" in his textbook on the social responsibilities of business. The pyramid can be thought of as a four-drawer file cabinet that both defines and describes a socially responsible business organization.

At bottom is the economic level—the organization must be economically viable if it is to be socially responsible. Hence, *profit* is not a dirty word. It is an essential element of social responsibility. I employ an analogy to make this point with students. Just as a human person cannot survive without food, a business firm cannot survive without profit. But who would seriously say that it is a good idea to maximize your intake of food? So when deciding what's best for a firm, you should work to optimize the firm's long-term viability, not make the mistake of thinking profit maximization is the way to make responsibility happen.

The second level of corporate social responsibility is the legal aspect. In the opening days of any college course in business ethics, a typical student will define business ethics as "making sure you operate within the law." But not all ethical requirements are mandated by law (nor are all unethical behaviors forbidden by law). So the legal aspect is an important element but the social responsibility story does not end there.

The third level—above the economic and the legal—is the ethical. This means doing the right thing. It marks the introduction of "ought" and "ought not" into managerial decisions and deliberations. The sources of ethical standards can be found in reason (through philosophical inquiry), in religion and revelation (through theological reflection), in experience (by a review of personal, vicarious, historical, literary experience), and in common sense (too often overlooked as an ethical standard). It is at this third level, the ethical, that considerations of character—what it is, how it is formed, and what strengthens or weakens it—enter the picture.

Fourth, at the top of the pyramid, is what Archie B. Carroll calls the voluntary/discretionary/philanthropic dimension of corporate social responsibility. At this level, the corporation does good things that are not necessarily profit producing. Nor are they required by law. Nor would one be considered unethical for omitting them. But they are good for the community and a good corporate citizen should be doing them—for example, helping the homeless, supporting the symphony orchestra, supporting both public and private education, doing volunteer community service on or off company time.

One of my Jewish friends, himself an admirably socially conscious citizen, insists that there is nothing "discretionary" about his philanthropic and volunteer activity. He subsumes it under the "ethical" and regards it as part of his Jewish cultural/religious responsibility. He considers himself thus obliged.

Within, and indeed through, this four-level framework, all of us should be looking at the real world of business and taking the measure of social responsibility in ourselves and our organizations.

73. Enron, Andersen, and Ethics

Representative James C. Greenwood, a Republican of Pennsylvania, chaired the investigative subcommittee of the House Energy and Commerce Committee when the Enron crisis surfaced. At a January 24, 2002, hearing, Mr. Greenwood said to David B. Duncan, the dismissed Arthur Andersen partner accused of orchestrating the destruction of documents in the case, "Mr. Duncan, Enron robbed the bank. Arthur Andersen provided the getaway car, and they say you were at the wheel." Mr. Duncan, on advice of his lawyers, asserting his Constitutional right under the Fifth Amendment, declined to reply.

It is always easy to substitute blame for analysis. There is more than enough blame to go around for the Enron collapse. Analysis is harder to come by.

In the wake of the bankruptcy, one Enron executive committed suicide, others resigned (presumably, to spend more time with their lawyers), some went to jail, thousands of employees lost their jobs, and even more were left holding empty 401(k) bags. Greed, deceit, mismanagement, and multiple conflicts of interest figured in all of this, as did the purchase of political influence in the soft-money swamp that will not be drained unless Congress imposes on itself serious campaign finance reform. This case also involved accounting fraud, insider trading, and illegal destruction of documents.

It is not enough to call this a "systemic" failure. Systems are made up of decision-making persons. In the Enron-Andersen debacle, human beings chose to act unethically.

Enron started out as a natural gas company. In an environment of deregulation, Enron became an unregulated energy contract trading company with relatively few real assets. If you are a trading company, all you really have is your credit. Enron lost both credit and credibility. It tried to hide its losses by inflating earnings reports and shifting debt from its balance sheet to newly created offshore partnerships. For the "system" to work, the public has to be able to trust the numbers. This means trusting those who post the numbers and those who certify them to be true.

The company failed to warn its employees of impending doom. In fact, it positively misled employees to believe the company was strong and prevented employees from selling the Enron stock in their 401(k) retirement plans (because the company switched plan administrators) at the same time that top executives of the company were unloading theirs.

Congress failed, under heavy industry lobbying, to pass laws that would prevent Enron from doing risky trading online that extended far beyond energy transactions. In fact, Congress in 1992 exempted Enron and other power marketers from oversight by the Commodity Futures Trading Commission. Congress also failed to respond to a plea from then chairman of the Securities and Exchange Commission, Arthur Levitt, Jr., to impose tough conflict-of-interest restrictions on accounting firms. Had Congress been able to resist pressure from lobbyists for the big accounting firms, it would have been illegal for Arthur Andersen, Enron's outside auditor, to be a paid consultant to the company it was also engaged to audit. In the year before the collapse, Andersen reportedly received from Enron twenty-seven million dollars in consulting fees while earning twenty-five million dollars as Enron's auditor.

Another fault, shared by the company and the Congress, was the failure to regulate the amount of Enron stock employees held in their retirement accounts. It is foolish to have your retirement assets in the stock of one company. By overloading their employees' defined contribution retirement plans with Enron stock (and encouraging the employees to buy more Enron stock themselves), the company shifted the risk involved in the retirement plan to the employee. There is a lesson to be learned here by those who think that individual Social Security retirement accounts should be privatized.

Ethics means doing the right thing. Enron took an end run around ethics as Andersen certified the company's questionable playbook. Now both are gone and we are left to wonder whether business and the bean counters are any the wiser as a result.

74. Secrecy, Easy Money, and the Violation of Trust

An invitation to Transparency International's Tenth Annual Anti-Corruption Conference (October 7–11, 2001, in Prague, Czech Republic) prompted me to recall a presentation I made to business leaders in Prague one year earlier. I spoke at a "Leadership Forum" involving faculty from the Georgetown Business School and Prague's Charles University, the Washington-based Woodstock Theological Center, and Czech business executives. My message in Prague was simple and clear; it was one I had communicated often to students when I taught in the business school at Georgetown University. There are three signs of graft— secrecy, easy money, and the violation of trust. There are also three degrees of graft—gift, bribe, and extortion.

Students in my course, "The Social Responsibilities of Business," always looked puzzled when, without any lead up to the question, I asked: "What is graft?" After a refresher note about skin grafts, botanical grafts, and other familiar "add on" or "extra layer" situations with which they were familiar, students recognized a connection between news accounts about police corruption, business bribery, and other shady dealings, and the "extra layer" features of familiar surgical grafting procedures. Business bribery, political and police corruption typically involve an unearned, unethical, and illegal "extra layer" of income lining the pockets of the wrongdoer.

My topic at the Prague conference was "Principled Leadership in Business." In the audience were Czech business leaders, happy but not yet fully at home in the free market system that emerged after the collapse of Communism in their country a decade earlier. Under the old system, one told me, there was a maxim followed by many: "He who does not cheat in business is stealing from his family." Corruption was widespread; so were inefficiency and economic stagnation.

Things were improving. But in the year 2000, the Czech Republic ranked near the middle among ninety nations on the "Corruption Perceptions Index" published by Transparency International. The list is based on perceptions of the degree of corruption as seen by business people, risk analysts, and the general public. (Finland and Denmark had the best ratings. Yugoslavia and Nigeria were at the bottom. Australia and the United States were, respectively, thirteenth and fourteenth from the top.)

Whenever you find secrecy, the prospect of making easy money, and a violated trust as part of the cost of doing business present in one combination, beware. The graft syndrome is taking shape.

The degrees of graft range from a gift (which obliges the recipient to reciprocate), to a bribe (which pays someone to do what should not be done, or not do what should be done), all the way to extortion (which is a hold up, a forceful demand to "pay up, or else"). Not all business or political gifts are wrong, but some are calculated to render the recipient not only grateful, but "much obliged" to do the bidding of the giver. Bribery is always wrong because it purchases the integrity of the person who, because of the pay-off, "looks the other way," or acts contrary to his or her contractual obligations. And, of course, the strong-arm extortion practices of purchasing agents, building inspectors, licensing bureaus, and others who abuse their positions of power are as well known as they are indefensible.

There is something here for everyone to consider. Secrecy doesn't always bring out the best in us. Easy money, easy pleasure, or easy advantage in competitive situations, often requires that you pay the price of diminished personal integrity. And any one of us is always capable of violating a trust. That's something to think about anytime in Prague or Peoria, or wherever you happen to be.

75. Workplaces Where It Just Doesn't Work Out

I've long entertained an organ-transplant theory to explain success or failure in hiring high-level academic executives.

A college or university board of trustees finds a vital, healthy "organ" (a strong candidate for president or provost, for example) and transplants it into the body academic, which, they sometimes forget, has an immune system called tenure. Unless the "organ," healthy at the point of transfer, can enculturate or acculturate to its new environment, a rejection mechanism can be triggered and soon the transplanted organ is gone!

There was nothing wrong with the replacement; he or she just didn't accommodate well to the new surroundings. Indeed, it is sometimes the case that the stronger and more vital the transplanted executive is, the quicker the rejection mechanism goes into play, if enculturation did not occur. The well-ensconced, long-tenured members of the academic community give, as it were, a collective thumbs down followed by an inhospitable boot out.

It may take a couple of years for this to happen, but it does every now and then, if the transplanted organ, healthy at the point of entry, fails to settle in.

This theory has helped me understand parallel situations in business, politics, and sports.

I found myself employing it again when I read of Michael Jordan's unceremonious ouster from the organization that owns the Washington Wizards. His playing days were, by his own decision, over. His transfer back into the management ranks of the sports enterprise that owned the team was, he thought, a slam dunk. But for reasons reminiscent of the rejection-mechanism activity in other organizational settings, this more than healthy organ was rejected.

It seems that Jordan, who joined the Wizards management team in January 2000 as president of basketball operations, let go all but one of the players he inherited, hired coaches who proved to be inept, suggested that his owner-employer was too old, and, after vacating his management post to start playing again for the Wizards in September 2001, spent much time publicly criticizing his teammates. This is not the recommended return route to front-office employment.

Team owner Abe Pollin's statement at the parting of the ways: "While the roster of talent he has assembled here in Washington may not have succeeded to his and my expectations, I do believe Michael's desire to win and be successful is unquestioned." Farewell with faint praise. Jordan is now free to search for success in other places. The same scenario has played itself out in countless organizational settings over the years.

Any organization, including the Church, might review its own history of hiring and appointments in the light of this organ transplant theory. It is hard to think of an organization better able than the Church to foster a congenial culture for "transplants" who are faith-committed servant leaders or willing associates ready to cooperate in mission.

We, who work for the Church, just have to believe what we preach and try to outdo one another in witnessing to the one-sentence summary of the mission of Christ, who "came, not to be served, but to serve, and to give his life as a ransom for many" (Mark 10:45). The pay's not much, we admit (although the retirement benefits are out of this world!).

Too bad that parishes and church bureaucracies have not yet mastered the art of welcoming well-prepared transplants into an accepting culture of love where the rejection mechanism is even less active than a Maytag repair man.

76. What Every Job Seeker Needs: "Diplomatic Persistence"

"Job Security Jitters" was the *Washington Post* headline describing the "office mood." It coincided with my visit to 40Plus of Greater Washington to discuss *Finding Work without Losing Heart*, my 1995 book on involuntary separation from managerial employment. Every year since then, the Washington chapter of 40Plus, a career transition support group, has had me in to talk to its members.

I brought with me a clipping from the *New York Times* reporting on "Workers Who Feel Discarded: The Emotional

Pain of Unemployment." I could just as easily have referred to a *Philadelphia Inquirer* headline: "Frustration Grows for Jobless"; subhead: "job losses show no sign of abating as more people become unemployed." Had I waited another week, I could have clipped this frightening headline from the *New York Times*: "Jobless and Hopeless, Many Quit the Labor Force."

News and opinion columns across the country are discussing layoffs and on-the-job insecurity. According to a survey of one thousand U.S. workers and their counterparts in fifteen other countries by Right Management Consultants, anxiety about layoff is higher among U.S. workers (26 percent) than all the other nations surveyed except Great Britain (27.5 percent). Workers were asked: "What is the possibility of you being laid off from your job during the next year?" Relatively little worry was reported in Italy, Norway, Belgium, Sweden, and Denmark; up there on the stress scale with the United Kingdom and the United States were Canada, Hong Kong, and Australia.

"Empowering experienced professionals for successful career transitions" is how 40Plus describes itself. "Whether out of work or seeking a career transition, this is not the time to go it alone. When you are over forty, a career transition has unique challenges. You need the knowledge and peer-to-peer support that only 40Plus can provide."

Neither the challenges nor the organization are altogether "unique." All ages, both sexes, and varying levels of skill and experience find embodiment in stressed human beings who know how it feels to be out of work and looking, or on the job and worrying about becoming unemployed. What all of them need to hear is this: Don't try to go it alone.

Networking is essential. So is spousal support or, if the job seeker is single, support from someone who really cares. The major obstacle is discouragement and the chief antidote to discouragement is persistence. Religious faith can help. Faith that God is at your side can shore up faith in yourself. Knowing yourself and knowing how to plug any holes in your education and experience to make yourself a better match for new opportunities is now your full-time job.

A deacon at the Walnut Creek Presbyterian Church in Walnut Creek, California, knows unemployment from personal experience. He runs a support group "with a bit of a twist." "Instead of working to help people find a job," he said, "we work on the emotional support of people so that they can more readily be able to find a job." He's using *Finding Work without Losing Heart* in weekly meetings with his group.

Join a group and be persistent. Torrey Foster, who ran a church-based support group in Cleveland, used to tell his job seekers to be "pushy," but always explained that what he meant by that was "diplomatic persistence."

77. A Question for Business Leaders

One way to stop a business leader, or any other kind of leader, in his or her tracks, say consultants Robert Goffee and Gareth Jones, is to ask: "Why should anyone be led by you?" That question is the title of an article these observers wrote for the *Harvard Business Review* in the year 2000.

"Without fail," say the authors, "the response is a sudden, stunned hush. All you can hear are knees knocking."

The question is a good one to put to anyone in a leadership position. How would a high school principal answer, a college dean or president, or an elected official, a military officer, a cardinal, bishop, or pastor? How about the "head of a household," a teacher, a coach? The reply has to be something more substantial than, "I've been assigned," or "I won the election," or "I own the business." Leadership implies voluntary followership. If you're the leader, why should I follow?

Goffee and Jones give a backward glance through history and acknowledge that there have been widely accepted leadership traits and styles. But they change over time. Today, they argue, the times call for leadership that displays the following four qualities:

> Leaders should let their weaknesses be known. By exposing a measure of vulnerability, they make themselves approachable and show themselves to be human.

> Inspirational leaders trust their intuitive ability to set the course and decide when the timing is right.

> They display "tough empathy," meaning that they empathize realistically with people and also care "intensely" about the work employees do.

> They capitalize on what sets them apart, on what is unique about themselves.

These leadership qualities are right for our times because leadership today, say these authors, has to adapt to "endless contingencies" while making decisions suited to a particular situation. They have to be "good situation sensors [able to] collect and interpret soft data."

I was impressed about thirty years ago when I heard Dennis Goulet, of the University of Notre Dame, remark that to be effective, a leader had to be "available, accountable, and vulnerable." I thought then and continue to believe these three qualities are completely Christian in orientation and uncommonly valuable for anyone courageous enough to adopt them as personal leadership characteristics. Don't bet, however, that they will appear in the next "Jesus as CEO" book.

Decades ago Dwight D. Eisenhower explained that, "the President does not lead by hitting people over the head. Any damn fool can do that....Leadership is by persuasion, education, and patience. It is long, slow, tough work." Eisenhower also defined leadership as "the art of getting someone else to do something you want done because he wants to do it." If Ike possessed the "sensor" that Goffee and Jones say belongs in today's leadership tool kit, he would make that, "he or she wants to do it." But aside from that, not much else in leadership literature seems all that new.

Why should knees knock when a leader is asked, "Why should anyone be led by you?" If the so-called leader has specialized in unavailability, unaccountability, and presumed invulnerability, the question could be quite discomfiting. Any leader who doesn't see leadership as "long, slow, tough work" will surely be stopped or stunned by the question.

Those in leadership positions should be wise enough to ask themselves why they are there. And those who constitute the followership can exercise their own quiet leadership by raising that question ever so gently whenever the opportunity occurs.

78. When CEOs Get into Trouble

I mentioned my organ transplant theory for the selection of university presidents in a previous essay. It's applicable as well to corporate CEOs. I'd like to think it has ecclesiastical relevance but, given the special nature of their areas of jurisdiction, bishops and those who appoint them tend not to think about it, which is not to say it offers no help in explaining tensions sometimes encountered by local ordinaries.

This theory is the lens through which I read the news stories several years ago about the fix the president of Harvard University found himself in. Everyone remembers the flap caused by his speculation that innate differences between the sexes, relative to quantitative aptitude, might explain the disparity in the numbers of males and females in mathematics and the physical sciences.

It would be difficult to find a more vital "organ" than former Treasury Secretary Larry Summers when he was named president of Harvard in 2001. Before a detour into government service, he was a distinguished professor of economics (and the youngest professor ever to be awarded tenure) at Harvard. Once transplanted as president back into the body academic, which, as I explained earlier, has an immune system called tenure, the healthy "organ" has to enculturate if it's going to function well in its presidential role. Given the strength of the academic immune system (read: given the importance of getting along well with the faculty), and acknowledging the possibility of a less than perfect enculturation, it is no surprise to see the activation of a rejection mechanism. This can happen at any college or university. It happens in business too. Whether the organ will survive the transplant and stave off (not just stare down) the pressure of a rejection reaction, depends on the organ's ability to become comfortably enculturated.

That's what Summers, through a string of apologies, a series of open meetings with faculty, countless private conversations with advisers, and much reading and reflection, tried to do. A personality transplant is not an option, so it remained to be seen whether he could change his style in order to be able to continue to do his job. He couldn't. He didn't. He was out in 2006. He came back in 2009, not to academe but to government, as a top economic policy adviser to President Obama. He now has bigger problems to solve and fewer people to please.

The theory is helpful in examining the ouster of Carly Fiorina as CEO of Hewlett Packard in 2005. Recruited from outside the company, she decided to depart from the traditional "HP Way." She forced the merger with Compaq with the unintended consequence of triggering a culture shift that eventually did her in. *Business Week* online advised her to "Cook up a comeback. This may seem harsh, but you blew it. Still you're not the first CEO to get fired. So fess up to your failures at HP, hire a spin doctor, and network your way back into a corner office."

That hasn't happened yet and is unlikely to happen unless she comes to understand that enculturation, not spin, is the issue she has to address.

It would be good for the Church, I think, if this dynamic, within appropriate canonical confines and with all due reverential regard for the role of the Holy Spirit, came into play in the selection of bishops.

Any bishop, veteran or newly appointed, would benefit

personally, and for the good of the Church, from reflection on events at Harvard and Hewlett Packard. Getting to know his clergy, religious, and lay leadership in the diocese is just as important for a bishop as becoming familiar with and winning the trust of faculty by a top academic executive. It's a big mistake to bypass them in a rush to "relate to the students," a mistake many bishops make by getting out and about in parishes without showing themselves willing to be available, accountable, and, even vulnerable, in contacts with their diocesan professionals.

79. Going for the Very Best

"The sky's not falling; it has already fallen," said Bill McGarvey, editor-in-chief of BustedHalo.com, an online Catholic magazine focusing on religion and spirituality for "seekers" in their twenties and thirties. He was speaking to the annual membership meeting of the National Leadership Roundtable on Church Management in late June 2007 at the University of Pennsylvania's Wharton School of Business. His topic was "Recruiting the Very Best for Church Service."

Where are they? How do you reach them? What do you expect them to do? These big questions were on the agenda of about one hundred fifty (a drop from earlier years) reflective Catholics, lay and clergy (including a dozen bishops), who meet annually to figure out ways to improve the quality of management in the Catholic Church in the United States. Founded four years earlier as a response to the public disclosures of widespread mismanagement in the Church associated with the clergy sex-abuse scandals, the Roundtable is grounded in love, loyalty, and fidelity to the

Church while operating under the assumption that better management is both desirable and possible.

Meeting at the Wharton School is their way of saying that they take management seriously. Bringing together lay Catholics, who constitute a management elite in the world of business, with Church professionals, who acknowledge the need for help in facing up to management challenges, is a sound approach to better management in the Church.

Drafts were circulated at this meeting of three "ethics and accountability" codes drawing from work initiated at past conferences and hammered out in the interim periods. Understood as "Standards for Excellence" the codes treat, respectively, of management practices in parishes, dioceses, and Catholic nonprofits. They were tested in some of the dioceses whose bishops participated in the Roundtable before being given wider circulation for use across the country. (Contact National Leadership Roundtable on Church Management, 1350 Connecticut Ave., NW, Suite 825, Washington, DC, 200036, 202-223-8962.)

"Give Us Your Best: A Look at Church Service for a New Generation" was the theme of this meeting. I participated in a panel discussion on "Retaining and Motivating the Very Best for Church Service." I found it ironic, I said, that after a previous panel discussion of the demographics behind the priest shortage, it became clear that women dominate the ranks of those who are staffing parishes and running religious education programs in the Church today. I pointed out the obvious fact that there has never been an ordained priest who was not the son of a mother and if the Church continues to let women go underappreciated and become further alienated, there will be further erosion of the support from a mother that most ordained priests will recall receiving when they thought about a vocation to priesthood.

From his flattened-out position beneath a fallen sky, Bill McGarvey would have an optimistic word to share. Repeating the saying that "all politics is local," he noted that the Church is local too. The Church should get itself closer to the "localities" where the young are—on the Internet, podcasting, blogging, social networking ("no one under thirty buys a newspaper these days").

I came away from the conference with the conviction that "better" is a goal without a goal line. We can all get better in management and all other aspects of ministry. Even the "very best" can get better, but we won't attract the very best for ordained and nonordained ministry until all of us notice that we should be paying more attention to getting better all the time.

That's why I placed this essay, admittedly covering a "Church" topic, at the end of this book, in the section devoted to "business." Business needs the Church, as earlier essays in this section suggest, if it is going to stay on the straight and narrow path. But the Church really needs business, if it is going to learn how to manage in order to minister more effectively.

Just as kids used to trade baseball cards, I would love to see Catholic bishops and Catholic CEOs trade business plans, strategic thinking, and best practices. What an exchange that would be!

But first they're going to have to get to know one another, respect and trust one another, lose all interest in trying to "lord it over" the other, drop the masks, get off whatever "high horses" the corporations or archdioceses may have provided for their basic transportation, and begin to form a working partnership.

I'll keep "looking around" for signs of something along these lines happening as part of our American experience.

Also by William J. Byron, SJ

Toward Stewardship (1975)

The Causes of World Hunger (editor, 1982)

The 365 Days of Christmas (1996)

A Book of Quiet Prayer (2006)*

Words at the Wedding (2007)*

Praying with and for Others (2008)*

*currently available